Regional Sea Kayaking Series

# Guide to Sea Kayaking in North Carolina

*The Best Day Trips and Tours from Currituck to Cape Fear*

by

Pam Malec

The Globe Pequot Press

Guilford, Connecticut

Cover photo: Kitty Hawk Sports
Cover design: Adam Schwartzman
Text design: Casey Shain
Maps: Dubé Studio

Photo credits: Pp. 1, 45, 47, 52, 68, 73, 78–79, 101, 114, 119, 149, 155, courtesy of Outer Banks Visitors Bureau; pp. 3, 36, 84, 90, 113, 118, 130, 138, 143, 163, by ArtToday; pp. 10, 34, 62, 94, 98, 104, 123, 129, 136, 172, by Mike Booher, courtesy of Outer Banks Visitors Bureau; pp. 11, 128, by Joy Hall; pp. 17, 22, 26, 67, 82, 86, 87, 109, 152, by Pam Malec, courtesy of Kitty Hawk Sports; pp. 21, 39, 106, 140, 145, 159, by Teresa Kelly; p. 169, by Shelley Wolf.

**Library of Congress Cataloging-in-Publication Data**
Malec, Pam.
    Guide to sea kayaking in North Carolina: the best day trips and tours from Currituck to Cape Fear / by Pam Malec—1st ed.
        p.   cm.   (Regional sea kayaking series)
    Includes bibliographical references.
    ISBN 0-7627-0817-4
    1. Sea kayaking—North Carolina—Guidebooks.   2.
North Carolina—Guidebooks.   I.  Title.   II. Series.
GV776.N74.M35        2001
917.5604'44—dc21
                                            2001018189
Manufactured in the United States of America
First Edition/First Printing

*Advance praise for*

# Guide to Sea Kayaking in North Carolina

"Very comprehensive and fun to read . . . a good guidebook that is so descriptive, so evocative, and so complete that you'll have trouble putting it down to actually go take a trip!"

—Joe Miller, Outdoor Columnist,
*The Raleigh News & Observer*

"Anyone who paddles along the North Carolina coast will cherish this guide. It's comprehensive, practical, informative, and easy to use. It's one of a kind."

—Mary Ellis, Editor,
*Our State Magazine: Down Home in North Carolina*

# Help Us Keep This Guide Up to Date

Every effort has been made by the author and editors to make this guide as accurate and useful as possible. However, many things can change after a guide is published—establishments close, phone numbers change, facilities come under new management, and so on.

We would love to hear from you concerning your experiences with this guide and how you feel it could be improved and kept up to date. While we may not be able to respond to all comments and suggestions, we'll take them to heart and we'll also make certain to share them with the author. Please send your comments and suggestions to the following address:

The Globe Pequot Press

*Reader Response/Editorial Department*

P.O. Box 480

Guilford, CT 06437

Or you may e-mail us at:

*editorial@globe-pequot.com*

Thanks for your input, and happy travels!

This book is dedicated to Ralph Buxton, Mary Jaslieum, Elaine Goodwin, Sandra Bull, and Teresa Kelly, and all the staff at Kitty Hawk Sports. The valuable experience I gained with all their help and support as Kayak Program Director helped make this book possible.

# NORTH CAROLINA

### Overview

# Contents

# Acknowledgments

Thanks to the many people who helped make this book possible. There have been so many who encouraged and motivated me, helped with the research, and just were there for silent support when I needed it.

To my children, Brian and Austin: Thanks for being so patient and understanding. While I've followed my heart, you've followed me down many paths and river banks and waited on many beaches. I love you.

To Rex Etheridge, John Jackson, Ken Jefferson, and John Rette— Team OBX: Thanks for all the support you've given me over the years in all my ideas and activities, and for just being the wonderful people you are.

To Teresa Kelly, contributing photographer: Thanks for your incredible patience, for your wonderful pictures, and for listening to all my tales, good or bad.

A big thanks to Barb Blonder, North Carolina Coastal Reserve; Bob Woody, U.S. National Park Service, Chief of Interpretation; and Bonnie Strawser; U.S. Fish & Wildlife, Alligator River National Wildlife Refuge, and Pea Island National Wildlife Refuge.

Thank you to my parents, who started all this by winning a kayak in a contest, and who always told me I could do anything I set my mind to do.

Thanks to Lafe Low, Jeff Serena, and all the staff at The Globe Pequot Press for making this first foray into publishing so enjoyable and rewarding.

# Introduction

There's something about the North Carolina coast that's unlike anywhere else in the world. This thin chain of barrier islands, called the Outer Banks, stretches more than 150 miles from the Virginia state line south to Cape Fear, near the South Carolina border. Used by many but tamed by no one, belonging more to the sea and wind than the land, these islands are made of many things: shifting sands, changing tides, violent storms, searing sun, salt spray, and the powerful sea.

It's not just one thing that makes the North Carolina coast special. It's the spring, when one day it can be calm and balmy and the next day the northeast winds can whip the ocean into a frenzy of near hurricane force. It's the summer, when you can play in the crystal clear ocean, paddle to a deserted island in the sound, explore hidden coves, or just lounge on the beach. It's the fall, when the light makes everything look golden and the crowds have gone. It's the winter, when you can have miles of beach to yourself. This is where stress dissolves, your body relaxes, your sense of wonder returns, and your smile is genuine. It's wild and untamed, calm and beautiful, exciting and relaxing, all at the same time. It's also where I call home.

I've put together thirty-five trips, which should be suitable for paddlers of all levels. Some of these can be linked together to form multinight expeditions or shortened for a lunchtime paddle. I've included general information, tips, and cautions to help you get the most from your trip. Throughout the book, you will find short sidebars on the history of the area, wildlife to be seen, or interesting local lore.

Although you don't need to be an expert to head out and enjoy this beautiful area, increasing your knowledge and gaining valuable experience can only further your enjoyment of paddling and make for a safe trip. Be aware of your skills and seek additional experience or training, if needed. There are many books on the market that do a great job of explaining proper paddling techniques. I have included an appendix on local tour guides, outfitters, and paddling schools to help you gather information when planning your trip.

There are many more trips than the ones I have included in this book—you could spend every day on the water and not run out of new places to see. I hope you'll find this guide full of useful information.

Maybe you'll be one of the many folks who come to visit and end up staying forever. I'll see you on the water.

# Choosing Your Equipment

Kayaks come in all sizes and styles. In researching this book, I used touring kayaks (with rudders), recreational kayaks (without rudders), sit-on-tops, canoes, a surf ski, and even an outrigger canoe. Give some thought to where you will be paddling so that you choose the right kayak to fit the conditions of the area and your skill level. Keep in mind what activity you will doing. If you are a bird-watcher or fisherman, you might want to choose a more stable boat. Tackling the surf, try a sit-on-top or shorter-decked kayak. For an extended day or multinight trip, you will want to pick a boat with plenty of storage.

Beginners might want to choose a recreational kayak or a sit-on-top. They require very little skill to learn to paddle and are very forgiving. They are usually shorter and wider than traditional sea kayaks, making them more stable. Recreational kayaks are primarily used for the more protected waters in mild to moderate wind conditions. The ones I used were approximately 12 to 13 feet long, without a rudder or a skeg. Recreational kayaks would be best used in the protected creeks and bays in fair weather and wind conditions of less than 10 knots.

Sea kayaks are a good choice when you will be going out in rough water, or with winds over 15 miles per hour. They are longer and narrower, which helps with turning and tracking. Most sea kayaks can be purchased with a rudder or skeg. Rudders and skegs are used for tracking and counteracting the effects of wind and tide. A rudder is mounted on the stern of the boat and is lowered by a cable or rope while you are paddling. You operate the rudder with your feet by using foot pedals. Skegs are used for the same reason as the rudder, but no foot pedals are used.

Although there is much controversy over using a rudder on your boat, in coastal North Carolina a rudder or skeg can make the difference between an enjoyable trip or a miserable day.

If you are staying mostly on open water, you will want a boat that will stay on a straight course for long distances. A kayak that can turn quickly in tight spaces is best for exploring the winding salt marsh creeks. To have the best of both worlds, try a boat 15 to 17 feet long.

You will also want to think about what material you want your kayak made of. The greatest majority of boats available on the East Coast are made of plastic. Plastic boats are very durable and relatively inexpensive. Fiberglass or other composite kayaks are also very popular. Their weight is their biggest selling point. A 17-foot plastic kayak will weigh about 60 pounds, while the same boat made of fiberglass is usually 40 to 50 pounds. A 17-foot kayak made of Kevlar will weigh only 30 to 35 pounds. The main factor in deciding what material you want, next to cost, is probably going to be transportation. If you paddle alone, make sure you can load and unload your boat yourself.

If possible, choose a boat with bulkheads. These compartments are usually waterproof and have hatches on the deck for easy access. They can be used to store gear, and they also serve to keep your boat buoyant if you should capsize. If your boat has no bulkheads, make sure you have flotation bags, which, when inflated, will help prevent it from sinking.

The deck of the boat should be equipped with deck lines. These lines go around the perimeter of the top deck. They are used for grabbing and maneuvering the boat during rescues. Some deck lines are made of bungees, which come in handy for holding down gear, maps, or other supplies.

In the cockpit of the boat, you will want to make sure you have foot pedals. These are used to rest your feet on for balance and are also used to operate the rudder.

There are many rental operations and outfitters up and down the Carolina coast. It is possible to rent most any type of paddle craft you could want. Quite a few of these stores are located on the water, eliminating the need to transport your boat, which is not always possible with a rental car. If you are in your own vehicle, most outfitters do provide foam blocks and straps to attach the boat to your car. Call in advance to determine which types of boats they carry and what other equipment is available. This could reduce your packing substantially, although you may also want to bring some of your own gear. I am used to my own paddle and PFD and always bring mine along. You will need to have a PFD on board, and I strongly recommend wearing it while in the boat. It is a North Carolina state law that you must have one on your boat at all times; you can be fined $100 if you don't.

Once you've decided on which boat to take, make sure you are outfitted with the proper gear for your trip.

Although most of these trips are within sight of land, always carry a compass when paddling coastal North Carolina. It can get foggy here, especially in the winter and spring. I have sometimes been unable to see land from just a few yards offshore. If you are crossing the wider part of the sounds, you can be out of sight of the land altogether. Make sure you know how to use a compass, and practice navigating before starting an extended trip, or even a short one if you are unfamiliar with the area.

In addition to your necessary paddle gear of paddle, PFD, and skirt, a bilge pump, paddle float, tow rope, whistle, and first-aid kit are highly recommended. If it's been a while since you've paddled, don't forget the moleskin for blisters. Insects are not usually a problem on most waterways, but due to the coastal breezes, some of the more protected areas could be miserable without insect repellent. Duct tape can come in handy, and you should bring a knife in case you snag your rudder in the remains of one of the numerous crab pots in the sound. Many of these are submerged and have been separated from their buoys. This can especially be a problem during low water days.

The sun can be intense here in the summer. Even on cloudy days, you can still get quite a burn. Always use sunscreen and bring a hat for shade. I like to bring a lightweight long-sleeved top to prevent over-exposure. Sunglasses, preferably polarized ones, can save your eyes from getting tired in the constant sun and wind. This can make you less tired and less likely to make mistakes of judgment. Always bring plenty of water to prevent dehydration.

Outfitters don't always provide safety gear. If you are renting, call in advance; if they don't have safety equipment available, bring your own. A few items you won't want to forget on a longer trip are:

- A wide-brimmed hat, with chin strap for windy days
- Seasonable, comfortable clothing
- Toilet paper
- Waterproof storage bags
- Maps of the area
- A repair kit

For shorter paddles you can use gallon-size plastic freezer bags for storage. They fit in the hatches of most boats more easily than the bulky dry bags.

Introduction

# Paddling the North Carolina Coast

Coastal North Carolina is a paddler's paradise. It has something for everyone, from the waves on the Atlantic to the calmer waters of the numerous sounds and creeks. You can spend days exploring the beaches and islands, or photographing the wildlife and scenery. You can paddle here in any season and most weather if you are prepared.

You will soon find out that the major factors to be mindful of while paddling in coastal North Carolina are the wind and the sun. The typical day on these barrier islands may start off sunny and mild with a light breeze blowing. A few hours later, the wind may switch from one direction to another and what you thought was going to be an easy paddle may turn out to be quite a struggle. Afternoon thunderstorms have been known to come virtually out of nowhere, with winds gusting up to 70 miles an hour. Lightning, waterspouts, and heavy rain can create very dangerous conditions. The sun can be intense, especially if the wind should stop. Damage to your skin and heat exhaustion or heat stroke can be prevented by planning ahead.

## Know Your Limits

Conditions can vary greatly in each location, even on the same day. There's a saying on these islands that if you want different weather, drive 5 miles. It can be raining on one side of the street and sunny on the other. Make sure you plan your trip accordingly and are confident enough of your skills before you take off. Although most of the trips are within sight of land, things can quickly get out of hand. The sounds behind the barrier islands can be very shallow, usually only a few feet. If the winds pick up, it takes only a few minutes for the water to go from flat to furious. Make sure you are able to cope with conditions that may arise. Above all, don't push it. If in doubt, choose a safer and more protected route.

## Get a Weather Forecast

Always check the weather before you go for wind direction, temperature, and any chance of thunderstorms. Accurate weather forecasts are available from the local radio and television stations. I highly recommend a portable weather radio to keep you up to date on your longer trips.

North Carolina has four very distinct seasons. Good paddling can be found year-round, but each season has its own rewards and cautions. Springtime is cool and windy. Strong storms from the northeast called "nor'easters" can blow for days. This pushes the water from the northern areas toward the south, resulting in very shallow or no water in some places and flooding in others. Keep an eye on your map and plan accordingly. Use the islands to help block the wind when planning your trip. Stay in the lee whenever possible.

Summer days are made for paddling. The wind is generally from the southwest and tends to pick up in the afternoon. Get out early and try to plan your trip so you paddle into the wind at first; if the winds do start to blow, you will get a little help on your return trip. An early start will also help keep you out of the heat of the day. Make sure you have a backup plan in case the afternoon turns stormy. No one wants to be caught off guard in the middle of the sound with a thunderstorm brewing. Afternoon is also prime time for waterspouts. The winds inside a spout can reach up to 150 miles per hour. You can usually spot them coming across the sound and move easily out of their way. If you can, get to shore. Although they resemble tornadoes, waterspouts usually dissipate when they hit land.

Fall is the best time to explore. The temperatures are still mild, usually around 80 degrees through mid-October. The water temperature is at its warmest, the crowds are gone, and rates for food and lodging are lower. Because this is prime hurricane season, you will still need to keep an eye on the weather. Warnings are given days in advance and you should have plenty of time to make arrangements for leaving if the need arises.

In the winter, the weather can be cold and windy. The Gulf Stream, which comes very close to the North Carolina coast, moderates the temperatures. Water temperatures drop to near 40 degrees and air temperatures at night can get down to 20 degrees. North of Oregon Inlet, it can be much colder than down around Wilmington. South of Frisco, the land is closer to the Gulf Stream and the water temperature can be a good 20 degrees warmer than in the northern areas. Winter is still a great time to explore, however. There is a clarity to the air that you don't see during the rest of the year. Many migrating birds spend their winters here, and there are so many secluded beaches that you can escape without going far. My favorite winter activity is paddling during the full moon. With good planning and cold-weather gear, there is no need to pack up your boat for the winter.

Cold-water paddling can be very enjoyable if you are properly dressed. The key to being comfortable and safe is to stay dry and warm. Although there are many wonderful, technical materials to help you do just that, you don't need to spend a fortune.

When dressing for cold-water kayaking, avoid cotton. It keeps you cool in the summer, but does not insulate or keep you warm. Stick to clothing that insulates when wet, such as fleece, synthetics, or wool. Choose clothing that can be layered for warmth and taken off easily when you get too hot. This will help you stay comfortable through the widest range of conditions. Your first layer, which lies next to your skin, should wick moisture away from your body. Pick a lightweight fabric of nonabsorbent material such as Capilene or polypropylene. The second layer should insulate, trapping the air warmed by your body. Fleece or wool is a good choice. Finally, the outer layer should protect and shield your body from wind and water. A waterproof shell that also breathes is preferable. Try to choose one with neoprene cuffs and neck to keep water out if you capsize. Round your outfit out with a warm hat of neoprene, fleece, or wool; gloves or poogies; fleece socks; and neoprene booties.

## Land Safely

Landing around North Carolina coastal waters is usually a simple matter. The shallow, sandy bottoms of most of the sounds make for easy entries and exits from your craft. Some areas have very soft, muddy bottoms. Most of these are located in the estuaries. If you find yourself in one of these spots at a time you just have to make a pit stop, test the bottom with your paddle before getting out. We have what is known as "sucking mud." Some call it "quickmud," others "slough mud." Whatever you want to call it, it's just not the ideal area to exit your kayak. You can sink in it to your hips, making life miserable for a while (and quite smelly too!). Exiting your kayak on the Atlantic side can be tricky. Try to plan your trip on the outside around good weather. Offshore storms can create large waves, which can make surf landings dangerous. On some beaches, the waves can throw you directly onto the beach, and I know of several folks with composite boats who were glad they had duct tape after such landings. Make sure your bracing skills and surf entries and exits are up to par before paddling on the ocean. No matter where you land, wear water shoes or sandals. Many hazards lie under the water, particularly on the sound side. Oyster shells can be razor sharp; broken glass, fishing hooks, and old crab pots can cause serious injuries.

## Camp Clean

Most of the camping areas mentioned in this book are primitive. There are some commercial campgrounds along the coast that are accessible from your kayak, but the majority are where you find them. Camping is not permitted in the U.S. Fish and Wildlife Reserves. Backcountry camping is permitted within the National Seashores, but you must be more than 1 mile off a paved road. You will have a hard time finding such a place on the northern barrier islands.

The best wild campsites remain the many offshore islands. Although they are privately owned, camping is allowed on most of them if you follow a few rules. Look for the white sand beaches with no homes in sight, and be discreet and quiet. Quite a few of the islands have fishing camps on them that are deserted most of the year. Respect the owner's privacy. If you see activity, either get permission to stay or move to another location.

Try to set up camp in the late afternoon out of sight of boat traffic. Keep your campsite clean and do not start a campfire. Remember, there is no water or shade on most of these islands so be prepared to pack everything in, and pack everything out. Strive for zero impact.

# Natural History

Few places are as dynamic as the Outer Banks. Barrier islands are the first line of defense for the mainland against the weather. These narrow islands lie a short distance offshore, where they protect the mainland and inland sounds and estuaries from storms and tides, much like a bumper protects a car. They formed about 17,000 years ago, at the end of the last Ice Age. The islands began to move south—as much as 50 miles—as rising sea level, winds, currents, and tides affected them. They are still moving today. Winds constantly blow sand from the shore to the sound. Storms open up inlets in one place and close them in another. Waves move the beach from north to south. Every year several homes are lost to seasonable wave action, and the coast has been badly damaged by hurricanes in the past few years.

The North Carolina coast is known for its wild beauty, remoteness, and history. As you paddle along, you will be surrounded by land with a long history of storms, piracy, shifting sands, almost constant wind, and most definitely beauty. Change is the essence of the North Carolina coast. Being prepared for change is the key to safely enjoying it.

The coast is part of the Atlantic flyway, the route many waterfowl use as they travel south for the winter. On any given day you may see swans, snow geese, Canada geese, and many different species of ducks, as well as egrets, herons, and other wading birds. The best place to see them in large numbers is in one of the many wildlife refuges. Ospreys, bald eagles, peregrine falcons, and species of hawks are seen regularly here. Ospreys are especially common. You can find their nests built on telephone poles, old bridge pilings, and trees. I've seen many flying off with a wriggling fish or snake between their talons.

Look for dolphins in the ocean just past the surf zone and in the sound along the deeper channels. They are most numerous from July through October, but can be seen at any time. It's thrilling to watch them, but the Marine Mammal Protection Act prohibits harassing, swimming with, or in any way endangering these marine creatures.

Sea turtles are common on the beaches in the late spring and summer. They come ashore to lay their eggs. If you are camping on the beach and happen upon one, don't bother it. Make note of its location and report it to the nearest wildlife officer or park office.

You may see alligators along the inland freshwater routes. These creatures are more shy than their southern relatives. They tend to dive into the water if you get too close. I don't know of any attacks by alligators upon paddlers, but use caution. They are wild and unpredictable.

On the ocean side look for huge manta rays leaping out of the water, their black wings spread until they land with a tremendous splash. The smaller stingrays can be found on the sound side. In the spring they migrate up the sounds to breed. If you are lucky, you may come upon a school of hundreds of them splashing around in the shallow water.

In summer, keep an eye out for jellyfish. The purple or white stinging nettle is the most common; the southern areas can harbor the Portuguese man-of-war. Meat tenderizer can take the sting out of the stinging nettles, but a run-in with a man-of-war may require medical assistance.

Snakes are everywhere here, both the poisonous and nonpoisonous varieties. Although you will see many water moccasins or cottonmouths, they don't usually bother people. Give them the right-of-way and don't splash or throw things at them. Just remember to keep your distance and you should not have any problems.

# How to Use This Guide

The trips are described starting from Currituck in the north and heading south to Cape Fear. A brief description of the area to be paddled will help to give you a little background on the trip. Each route is accompanied by a map of the area. The maps show the best way around the islands and marshes, but are not the only way through. Feel free to explore on your own, but make sure you bring a compass and map. These marsh mazes can be very tricky. *Caution:* Some of the creeks could be very shallow during high wind days.

The following information is provided for each route:

**TRIP HIGHLIGHTS:** This section provides a brief list of the area's main attractions.

**TRIP RATING:** The trips in this book are rated as *beginner, intermediate,* or *advanced.* The ratings are based on a variety of factors, including the overall mileage and duration of the trip as well as the hazards likely to be encountered. Hazards may include boat traffic, ferry wakes, inlet crossings, nearby shoals, strong tidal influences, exposure to wind, and remoteness of the final destination.

Additionally, the level of expertise needed depends on the weather and water conditions during your trip. I cannot stress enough the changeability of the weather on the North Carolina coast. It is very important to make sure you have the skills necessary to cope with adverse conditions. Only you know your limits. Expert instruction is available from a wide range of outfitters around the country. It is wise, regardless of your experience level, to contact a local shop or outfitter to find out as much about the area's quirks as you can before you plan your trip. You should also check the marine forecast before each trip to assess the weather and water conditions.

***Beginner:*** I categorize a beginning paddler as someone having a basic working knowledge of common paddle strokes and braces. You should be able to perform a self-rescue and an assisted rescue (such as the T rescue). You should be comfortable paddling in mild conditions with winds up to 10 knots, and for up to four hours at a time.

***Intermediate:*** As an intermediate paddler, you should be comfortable paddling in winds up to 20 knots, in waves 2 to 4 feet, and be able to paddle up to 20 miles per day in good weather. You should be proficient in self-rescue and group-rescue techniques, have good bracing skills, and be able to perform an Eskimo roll.

***Advanced:*** You should be comfortable paddling in winds up to 30 knots, and waves 5 to 6 feet in height. You should have strong bracing and paddling skills and be able to paddle in very rough conditions. You should be able to paddle up to 30 miles per day in good weather and have mastered self- and group-rescue skills. Advanced paddlers should be highly proficient navigating with a map and compass and possess good first-aid skills.

**TRIP DURATION:** You can spend a few hours or days in a particular area. Most of the trips I've included are four to five hours long. This should give you adequate time to relax, explore, eat lunch, take a nap, whatever. Those who wish a longer trip may link several areas together.

**NAVIGATION AIDS:** You can order National Oceanic and Atmospheric Administration (NOAA) charts directly from Distribution Division (N/ACC3), National Ocean Service, Riverdale, MD 20737-1199; (301) 436–6990 or (800) 638–8972.

Topographical maps are made by the U.S. Geological Survey. They are available from various marina stores or directly from the U.S. Geological Survey, Denver, CO 80225 or Reston, VA 22092. You will need to order them by name and scale, 1:24,000 or 1:100,000.

While the USGS maps and NOAA charts are good in some areas, I've found that the detail for the different areas are better on the local maps. The best ones I've found come from the various visitor centers, chambers of commerce, or real estate offices. Local maps are also available from ADC, 6440 General Green Way, Alexandra, VA 22312-0510; (703) 750–0510.

*Introduction*

**TIDAL INFORMATION:** Make sure you have a copy of the local tide charts. Planning your trip around the tides is wise, especially if you will be navigating inlets, exploring the shallow sound-side marshes, or going surf kayaking. Tide charts are available in tackle shops, in most local phone books, and in visitor guides.

**CAUTIONS:** Included are hazards you may encounter en route, such as submerged rocks, deep mud, strong currents, or dangerous wildlife.

**TRIP PLANNING:** This section includes tips to make your trip more enjoyable, such as what time of day is best, what wind direction is preferable for a particular route, or which time of year is best for visiting.

**LAUNCH SITE:** Directions from the nearest roadway to the launch site are provided. I recommend getting a good road map or gazetteer for ground directions. Gazetteers are available for most areas from Delorme Mapping, P.O. Box 298, Freeport, ME 04032; (207) 865–4171. I also include any fees, rest room facilities, and other information that may come in handy.

**DIRECTIONS:** A mile-by-mile description of the route includes interesting things to find, wildlife that may be visible, good photographic opportunities, and side-trip options. *Note:* The mileages given in the text are in statute miles, not nautical miles; 1.15 statute miles equal 1 nautical mile.

**WHERE TO EAT & WHERE TO STAY:** This section gives information on the closest and best places to eat, stay, or camp.

*Introduction*

# Map Legend

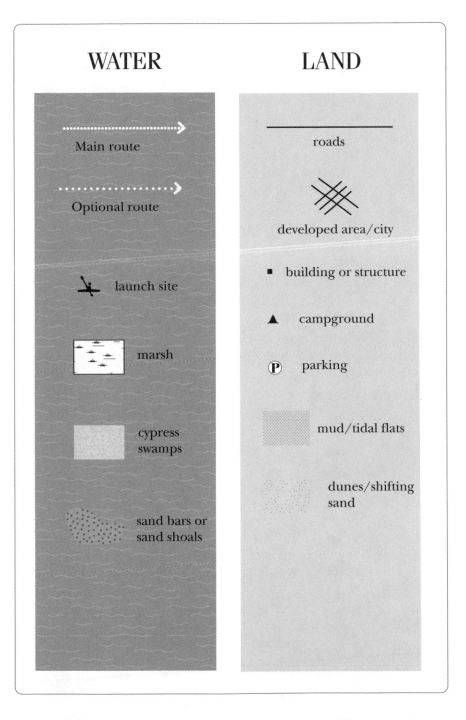

**WATER**

- ·····················> Main route
- ·····················> Optional route
- launch site
- marsh
- cypress swamps
- sand bars or sand shoals

**LAND**

- —————— roads
- developed area/city
- ■ building or structure
- ▲ campground
- Ⓟ parking
- mud/tidal flats
- dunes/shifting sand

# The Currituck Banks

# Route 1:

-- -- -- -- -- -- -- -- -- -- -- -- -- ➔

## *Whale Head Bay to Monkey Island*

**L**ike so many areas on the North Carolina coast, there is a story behind how Whale Head got its name. Legend has it that a very large whale washed up on the shore here many years ago. It is said that the whale was so big that you could drive a horse and buggy into its mouth. Whale Head Club was built by a gentleman named Edward Knight in 1920. He and his wife loved to hunt, but most hunting clubs did not allow women, so Edward built a club just for her. When complete, it had thirty-five rooms, copper shingles on the roof, and cork floors. Today, Whale Head Club is owned by Currituck County and managed by the Whale Head Preservation Trust.

The area around Whale Head Bay is known for its beautiful marshes, which are filled with wildlife such as otter, deer, and birds. It is well protected from the winds if you stay inside the islands. If you visit during the summer, look for dolphins in the water.

**TRIP HIGHLIGHTS:** Protected shallow water, wildlife, scenery, and bird-watching.

**TRIP RATING:** Intermediate. This is an easy trip if the wind is light. The outer islands tend to create a windbreak if there is any breeze.

**TRIP DURATION:** Part day or full day; 7 miles. The optional route is 8.5 miles.

**NAVIGATION AIDS:** ADC Map of the Outer Banks.

**TIDAL INFORMATION:** No tidal influence. The wind affects the water depth here. Don't plan on heading out if the wind is from the northeast at anything greater than 20 miles per hour. Northeast winds tend to blow all the water out of this area and it would be difficult to paddle in most of the areas.

**CAUTIONS:**   Watch out for evening thunderstorms, which tend to pop up suddenly. They pass through very quickly, bringing high winds and dangerous lightning. Keep an eye on the weather and head toward shelter at the first sign of an approaching storm.

**TRIP PLANNING:** The best time to paddle this area is in the morning when the wildlife is most active. Evening paddles are very enjoyable too, but watch for fast-moving storms.

**LAUNCH SITE:**   From NC–12 in Corolla continue north past Corolla Light shopping center. Turn left at the Whale Head Club entrance. Follow the road 0.25 mile to the public boat ramp. There is free parking at the boat ramp located just to the right of the Whale Head Club. It is a short distance from the water; unload your boat next to the ramp and then park your vehicle. In the warm summer months, the weeds can be very thick in the water here. It is a good idea to wait to put your rudder down until you clear the launch area.

**DIRECTIONS:**

**START:** Launch from the public boat ramp and head north (right), following the shoreline. *Caution:* Watch for thick sea grass and boat traffic during the summer months. Do not block the ramp with your kayak.

**MILE 0.75: Deep Creek,** a little creek on the right, is great for bird-watching or crabbing.

**MILE 1.0:** You will know you have reached **Jones Point** when you see a wide expanse of water directly ahead of you and a small island just behind you and on your left. From here you will head northwest. Head for Mary Island just ahead of you and on your left.

**MILE 2.0: Mary Island** is 0.5 mile long. Once you reach its northernmost point, you will be able to see Monkey Island. There is an old water tank and lodge on the island that stand out. Head northwest toward Monkey Island across Currituck Sound.

**MILE 3.0:** Once you reach **Monkey Island,** you can go around it in either direction. Circle the island, staying close to the shore. *Caution:* **Do not land on the island.** Mackey Island National Wildlife Refuge, the management for the island, has closed all portions of the island to the public. You can look, but don't get out of your boat. The northernmost portion of the island is one of the largest rookeries for egrets in North Carolina. The island was also used as a burial ground for the Pamonky Indians prior to settlement of the area.

**MILE 4.0:** Once you have circled the island, you can either retrace your path back to the takeout or take the optional route back.

**OTHER OPTIONS:** From Monkey Island, head directly east toward the Outer Banks. This route will add an extra mile to your return trip, but it is a more protected area to paddle if the weather turns bad.

**MILE 5.0:** Enter **Ships Bay.** Take time to poke around here for great bird-watching, crabbing, fishing, or photography. Follow the shoreline from Ships Bay south.

**MILE 6.0:** Turn left (east) into **Raccoon Bay,** another good spot for just meandering in the marsh. Keep an eye out for the local wildlife on the shore, such as raccoons, otters, nutrias, and snakes. Paddle southwest out of Raccoon Bay.

**MILE 7.5:** At Jones Point, turn left and retrace your original route for 1 mile to return to the launch site at Whale Head.

*Whale Head Bay to Monkey Island*

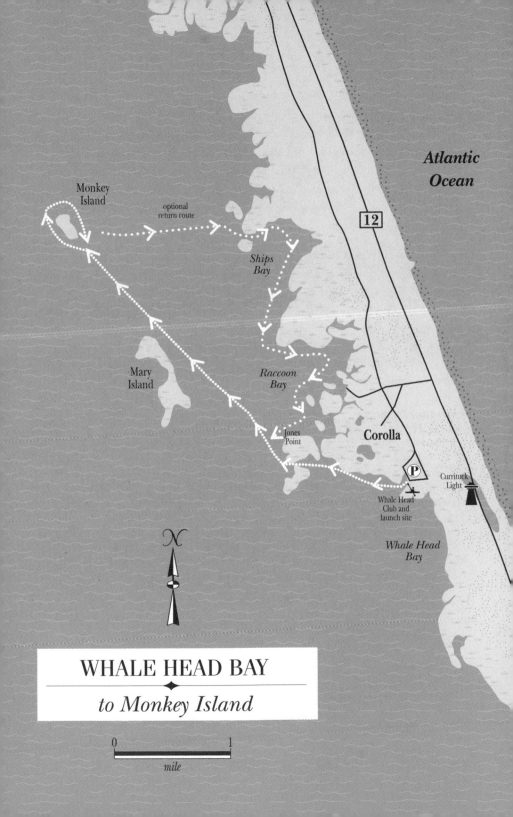

Atlantic Ocean

Monkey Island

optional return route

Ships Bay

12

Mary Island

Raccoon Bay

Corolla

Jones Point

P

Currituck Light

Whale Head Club and launch site

Whale Head Bay

N

WHALE HEAD BAY

to Monkey Island

0        1

mile

# Currituck Lighthouse

Currituck Lighthouse, the last lighthouse to be built on the North Carolina coast, sits next to the Whale Head Club in Corolla. It was commissioned in 1873 because so many ships and lives were being lost along the coast between the Cape Henry Light in Virginia and the Bodie Island Light in Nags Head. Completed in 1875, the lighthouse is 158 feet tall and was made with roughly one million bricks. Its light flash cycle—on for 3 seconds, off for 17 seconds—can be seen for up to 18 nautical miles.

Two keepers and their families used to share the keeper's house, but the keepers were no longer needed after the lights were automated in 1939, and the house was left empty. The Outer Banks Conservationists, Inc. has restored the Keeper's House, which is now open to the public twelve days a year. The lighthouse is open from late March through Thanksgiving, weather permitting.

## Where to Eat & Where to Stay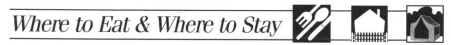

**RESTAURANTS** Try the *Weeping Radish Brewery* (252–453–6638) if you want a light meal. They brew their own beer, the famous Weeping Radish Beer; if you like dark beer, you've got to try the Black Radish Brew. Open year-round, it serves only lunch in the off-season. Follow Route 12 south to the Monterey Plaza.

**LODGING** Unless you are renting one of the megahouses for the week, you will have a hard time finding lodging in Corolla. The *Inn at Corolla Light* (252–453–3340) is within walking distance of Whale Head on Route 12. Very nice.

**CAMPING** See Route 5, Kitty Hawk Woods Preserve, for closest camping, or contact the Cape Hatteras National Seashore at (252) 473–2111.

*Whale Head Bay to Monkey Island*

# Route 2:

━ ━ ━ ━ ━ ━ ━ ━ ━ ━ ━ ━ ➤

## *Corolla Marshes from Timbuc II*

**C**urrituck first became known as the duck hunting capital of the East Coast. The name Currituck comes from the Indian word for "land of the wild goose." There used to be so many birds that they darkened the sky when they flew. Starting in the late 1800s, travelers started to come to Currituck to hunt the large number of ducks, geese, and swans. Local hunters, called market hunters, used a "punt gun," which resembled a large shotgun. It would hold a half cup of gunpowder and a full cup of shot. The hunters would first bait the area with corn, then return after dark with a special boat, a small skiff with a cover on it. The gun was mounted on top of the deck so the spray from the gun would be level with the surface of the water, allowing a hunter to kill hundreds of birds with one shot. The birds would be packed in barrels and shipped off to the large cities to be enjoyed by diners. This wholesale hunting decimated the number of waterfowl in the area. You won't see as many types of waterfowl today, but this trip will allow you to see what is still around. Keep an eye out for the other local wildlife such as snakes, turtles, white-tailed deer, and other small mammals.

**TRIP HIGHLIGHTS:** Protected creeks and sound islands; wildlife, including otter during the summer months.

**TRIP RATING:** Beginner.

**TRIP DURATION:** Three to four hours; 7 miles.

**NAVIGATION AIDS:** ADC Map of the Outer Banks.

**TIDAL INFORMATION:** The water level is not affected by the lunar tides, but rather by the wind tides. The best wind direction for this trip is west of southwest. A south wind pushes water into this portion of the sound.

**CAUTIONS:** Sun and wind remain the two great cautions here. Make sure you bring adequate sun protection and plenty of water to drink.

**TRIP PLANNING:** Check the weather before heading out. Large thunderstorms with high winds and dangerous lightning are frequent in the summer afternoons, and you may not always see them coming. Also bring plenty of water and sunscreen. It is easy to dehydrate in the sun here, especially if you are not used to it.

**LAUNCH SITE:** From NC–12 in Corolla, heading north, take a left into Timbuc II shopping center, which is located across the street from the Monterey Shores Food Lion shopping center. Continue to the back of the parking lot to the soundfront. Park in front of Kitty Hawk Watersports. Follow the boardwalk from the parking area down to the water. The boardwalk is about 100 yards long, so bring a boat tote if you have one. Once at the water, there is a floating dock from which you can launch. Ask permission first because the launch is private property. *Note:* During the summer months, expect lots of Wave Runner traffic if you head north. Stay to the south for peace and quiet.

## DIRECTIONS:

**START:** From the dock, which is located in **Sanders Bay,** head south (left) staying as close to the shore as possible. This is where you will see the most wildlife.

**MILE 0.5:** A left here will lead you into a small creek. It is 0.15 mile long and is worth the time because it is filled with birds, nutrias, and otters.

**MILE 1.5:** Stay to the left of the island directly ahead of you **(Buzzard Island).** A creek just past this point, on your left, is a good place for spotting wildlife.

**MILE 2.25:** Turn left into **Beasley Bay.** Stay as close to the shore as the water depth will allow. Depending on the tide, the water may be deep

*Corolla Marshes from Timbuc II*

launch site

Timbuc II
Shopping
Center

P

boardwalk

*Sanders
Bay*

*Atlantic
Ocean*

Mossey Islands

*Dotty
Pond*

12

Sanders Creek

Buzzard
Island

*Ware Creek*

*Piney
Cove*

*Beasley
Bay*

N

Hog
Islands

# COROLLA MARSHES

## *from Timbuc II*

0                                    1

*mile*

enough for you to explore the full length of the creek, which is about 1 mile round-trip. This is a good location for seeing the local population of white-tailed deer.

**MILE 3.75:** Look for the small islands on your right, known as the **Hog Islands,** and paddle until you are almost to the southern end, then turn around and retrace your route.

**MILE 5.5:** You will see the island you went around on the trip down the coast. Pass on the left side of Buzzard Island on your way back.

**MILE 7.0:** Return to the dock and launch site.

# Wild Horses

For hundreds of years, wild horses have roamed these islands freely. Legend has it they were put off Spanish ships that ran aground in the "Graveyard of the Atlantic." The horses swam ashore, and they've remained here ever since. You'll see them grazing on the grass at the Monterey Shores shopping center, nibbling at the fruit stand in Timbuc II, and walking along the beach. Although it is wonderful to see the horses roaming free, homeowners complain that they ruin their plants and endanger visitors and themselves. More than a dozen of them have been killed by vehicles while crossing the highway. For their own safety, a fence was put up from the ocean to the sound to control their wandering. This effort failed when ten horses just waded into the sound, swam around the fence, and continued to roam the streets. These escapees were relocated to homes on the mainland, and the remaining forty or so were left to roam safely behind the fence.

If you wish to see the horses today, you may visit the two-acre paddock at the Currituck Beach Lighthouse. Each Tuesday amd Thursday during the summer season, the Corolla Wild Horse Fund sponsors a talk on the history of the wild horses at the lighthouse. Several of the mares are kept penned there with their young. You might also chance upon any number of wild stallions coming to visit the mares. If you do see some of these horses wandering, please remember they are wild animals. They will kick and bite, so be sure to keep your distance.

# Where to Eat & Where to Stay

**RESTAURANTS**    You can take your pick of eating establishments at Timbuc II shopping center, which has everything from take-out steamed shrimp to a full-course dinner or lunch. *Steamers Shellfish to Go* (252–453–3305) features steamed seafood, great wraps, soft drinks, and wine. *Leo's Deli & Baked Goods* (252–453–6777) has sandwiches, salads, subs, desserts, drinks, and ice cream. *Grouper's Grille & Wine Bar* (252–453–4077) serves free-range chicken, Angus beef, local seafood, and vegetarian entrees; menu changes seasonally. **LODGING** Lodging in Corolla is not cheap. Plan on staying on the southern end of the Outer Banks and making this a day trip if you want to save money. The *Inn at Corolla Light*, 3 miles north of Timbuc II on Route 12, is very nice. For reservations, phone (252) 453–3340 or (888) 546–6705. To rent a house for the week, call *B&B on the Beach* at (252) 453–3033 or (800) 962–0201 (www.bandbonthebeach.com) or *Village Realty* at (252) 453–0409 or (800) 548–9688 (www.villagerealtyobx.com). **CAMPING**    The closest camping is located in Kitty Hawk at the *Outer Banks Hostel and Campground* (252–261–2294), 16 miles south of Timbuc II shopping center. Follow NC–12 south 15 miles to the intersection with U.S. 158 and take a right. Follow for 1 mile and take a left at Woods Road (NC–1206). Continue for just under 2 miles and take a right on Kitty Hawk Road West. The campground is 1 block on your right. It's open all year.

# Route 3:

▬▬ ▬ ▬ ▬▬ ▬▬ ▬▬ ▬▬ ▬ ▬ ▬ ▬ ▬ ▬ ➤

## Pine Island Audubon Sanctuary from Sanderling

**P**ine Island Audubon Sanctuary is a 5,000-acre wildlife sanctuary. Three miles long, it carries a variety of wildlife within its borders. Within this protected habitat you may see birds, deer, rabbits, and lots of plant life. You can walk through this sanctuary, but the best way to see all it has to offer is by a kayak. Marshland, dune habitat, maritime forest, and fresh and brackish water come together to create a diverse mix.

From the sound side you can explore the many marsh islands and narrow creeks. The sanctuary is protected from the northeast winds, which makes for easy fall and winter paddling. Fall is one of the best times to visit. The hardwood trees show their beautiful fall foliage and the migrating waterfowl are an amazing sight.

**TRIP HIGHLIGHTS:** Peaceful and quiet, protected from the wind, great for birds and fall foliage.

**TRIP RATING:** Beginner to advanced. A high level of paddling skill is not necessary if the conditions are good. Most of this area is protected from winds. A northeast wind will blow water out of the sound and make some areas impassable due to low or no water.

**TRIP DURATION:** Four to five hours; 8.5 miles.

**NAVIGATION AIDS:** ADC Map of Currituck County.

**TIDAL INFORMATION:** The tide here is not a factor.

**CAUTIONS:** Evening thunderstorms are common here. Make sure you check the weather before starting your trip.

**TRIP PLANNING:** Avoid this trip in times of high northeast winds.

**LAUNCH SITE:** From NC–12 heading south, turn right into the Sanderling Racquet and Swimming Club, 0.5 mile south of the Currituck/Dare county line. There is a nice ramp with a wooden pier to launch from. The sandy bottom makes for easy entry and exiting your kayak. *Note:* If the wind is from the northeast at more than 15 miles per hour, the water will be extremely low and you will have to walk your kayak out quite a ways to find water deep enough to paddle.

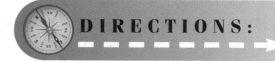

# DIRECTIONS:

**START:** From the ramp you will be able to see Flag Island, which is 0.5 mile from the launch, straight ahead. Paddle toward it.

**MILE 0.5:** At **Flag Island,** head to your right (northwest) and paddle past **Sedge Island.** Keep Sedge Island on your left and keep heading northwest.

**MILE 1.0:** Pass between the next two islands, through an area called **The Lead.** Continue northwest.

**MILE 1.5:** At **Sprig Point,** turn right and paddle north for 1 mile, passing through **Pine Island Bay.** Keep the continuous stretch of marsh grass on your right.

**MILE 3.0:** Paddle north through **Pine Island Lead.** (For a shorter trip, you can turn around here and retrace your path 3 miles back to the launch site.)

**MILE 3.75:** Pine Island Lead intersects with **Baums Creek.** Turn right and follow the shoreline down **Baums Lead.**

**MILE 4.5:** Continue following the creek to the right as it winds back toward Pine Island Bay.

**MILE 5.25:** Once you reach open water, turn left (south) and retrace your route to the launch site.

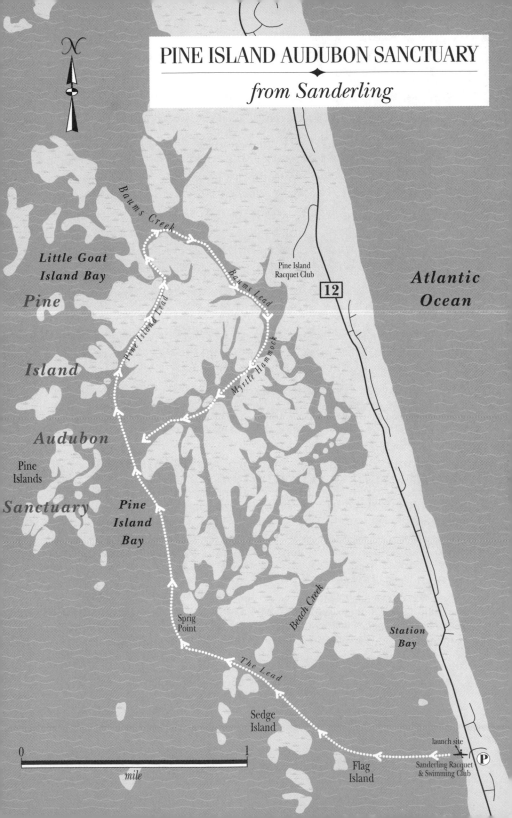

# PINE ISLAND AUDUBON SANCTUARY

## *from Sanderling*

N

Atlantic
Ocean

Little Goat
Island Bay

Pine

Island

Audubon

Pine
Islands

Sanctuary

Baums Creek

Baums Lead

Pine Island Lead

Pine Island
Racquet Club

12

Myrtle Hammock

Pine
Island
Bay

Sprig
Point

Beach Creek

Station
Bay

The Lead

Sedge
Island

Flag
Island

launch site

Sanderling Racquet
& Swimming Club

P

0        1
mile

# Wax Myrtle

If you paddle the protected coastal creeks of North Carolina, you will most likely run into the wax myrtle. This evergreen shrub lines the banks of most of the tidal creeks of the maritime forests. It stands up to 3 feet high and has smooth gray-green bark. If you take a close look at the shrub you will notice that the stems are covered with small, grayish white berries. The white substance on them is wax, which gave the shrub its name. Years ago, folks used to gather the berries in large numbers and boil them. The wax that melted off the berries would then be skimmed off the surface of the water and made into candles. The wax myrtle is related to the bayberry shrub, whose berries are used to make bayberry-scented candles.

Wax myrtle leaves are also useful as an insect repellent of sorts. If you are ever caught where the mosquitoes are bad, crush a handful of leaves (if you are sure you are not allergic to them) and rub them on your skin. (Note: Although this seems to work on mosquitoes, it just seems to make the biting flies mad.)

## Where to Eat & Where to Stay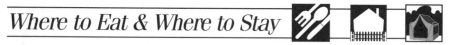

**RESTAURANTS**    For the best food around, try the *Sanderling Inn Restaurant* (252–453–1549). This restored lifesaving station offers regional cuisine. Open daily year-round for breakfast, lunch, and dinner. It's within walking distance of both launch sites. For something quick, try *Duck Seafood Buffet* (252–261–3901), 4 miles south of Sanderling Resort on NC–12.    **LODGING**    *Sanderling Inn Resort*, NC–12, Duck (252–261–4111 or 800–701–4111, www.sanderlinginn. com). *Advice 5 Cents*, a bed-and-breakfast in Duck (252–255–1050 or 800–238–4235, www.outerbanks.com/advice5).    **CAMPING**    The closest campground is *Outer Banks International Hostel* (252–261–2294, www.hiayh.org) on West Kitty Hawk Road in Kitty Hawk. In addition to camping they offer rooms for $18 a night.

# The Outer Banks

# Route 4:

---------->

## Martins Point and Duck

**W**hen Sir Walter Raleigh sent his ships to colonize the new world, they probably entered through an inlet between what is now Duck and Martins Point. Opinions vary, but many signs point to this area. Written accounts describe Jean Guite Creek as running parallel to the beach and opening up into a harbor deep enough for sea vessels.

All of what is now Southern Shores was once sand dunes and beach covered with dead cedars. Down Jean Guite Creek, however, was a thriving maritime forest. Live oaks big enough for ship timbers were cut, and a network of railway tracks was laid to move the lumber out of the Kitty Hawk Woods to the harbor for transport. Paddling from Duck to Martins Point, it is easy to see the change from beach to marsh to forest.

Although the area is now well populated, it is still a pleasant place to paddle. Martins Point is a gated community with well-appointed homes. Southern Shores contains hundreds of homes and a warren of canals to explore. The homes have not hurt the natural beauty of the area or chased away the many ducks, geese, and swans. White-tailed deer are common, as are snakes and many songbirds. This is a beautiful trip to take in the fall when the trees are changing color.

**TRIP HIGHLIGHTS:** A unique area to view three very different ecosystems as they flow into one another: the beach/dune, salt marsh, and maritime forest.

*Martins Point and Duck*

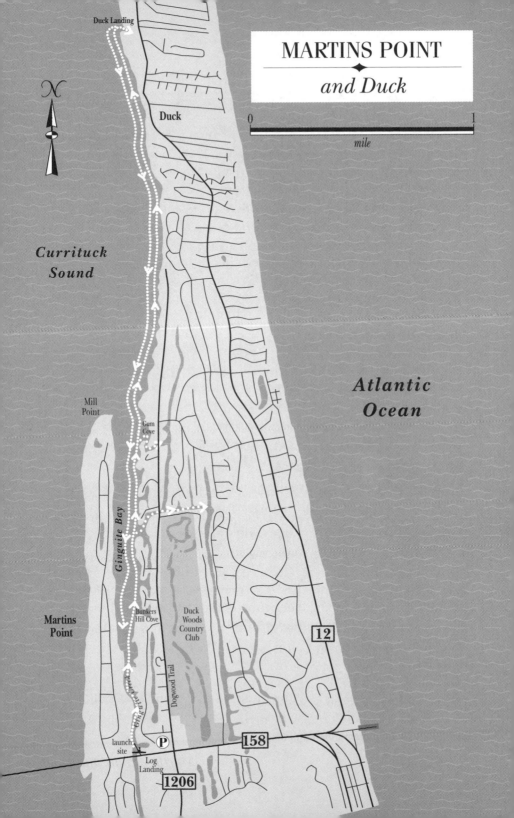

MARTINS POINT
and Duck

0                  1
*mile*

N

Duck Landing

Duck

*Currituck
Sound*

Mill
Point

Gum
Cove

*Atlantic
Ocean*

*Ginguite Bay*

Martins
Point

Bunkers
Hill Cove

Duck
Woods
Country
Club

Dogwood Trail

Ginguite Creek

launch
site

P

Log
Landing

12

158

1206

**TRIP RATING:** Intermediate.

**TRIP DURATION:** Five to six hours; 11 miles.

**NAVIGATION AIDS:** ADC Map of the Outer Banks.

**TIDAL INFORMATION:** No tidal influence due to distance from inlet.

**CAUTIONS:** There is some boat traffic here, so keep an eye out for them and try to get out of their way. Although nonmotorized boats have the right of way, I yield to bigger boats.

**TRIP PLANNING:** Try this route on a day with a light wind, preferably less than 15 knots. The canals are easy to paddle in, but the center of the Jean Guite Creek (maps have it listed as Ginguite Creek) and Ginguite Bay can be choppy in higher winds. Located at the launch site, Kitty Hawk Kayaks (a division of Kitty Hawk Sports) is the original kayak company on the Outer Banks and can provide you with advice, maps, and gear.

**LAUNCH SITE:** Follow U.S. 158 to milepost ¼. (The Wright Memorial Bridge starts at milepost 0 and goes up as you head south.) Look for a kayak shop (Kitty Hawk Kayaks) between a flag shop and a Chevrolet dealership on the south side of the highway. Unload your kayak in front and carry it to the launch site in back of the shop. There is no fee but ask permission before you launch.

# DIRECTIONS:

**START:** Once you leave the launch site, paddle north on **Jean Guite (Ginguite) Creek.** After a few yards you will pass under U.S. 158.

**MILE 0.5:** This is where the infamous "attack swans" hang out (see sidebar). Give them plenty of distance if you don't want a run-in with the male. He can be very intimidating, to say the least, as he rushes toward you with his wings flapping. Stick to the right of the creek in **Bunkers Hill Cove,** to bypass him and his girl.

**MILE 0.75:** Jean Guite Creek merges with **Martins Point Creek** and starts to widen. *Caution:* Keep your eye out for boat traffic during the busy summer months.

**MILE 1.5:** There is a canal on your right that you can follow through the residential area here. It is a nice side trip and the woods along the shore are filled with many types of birds.

**MILE 2.25:** You can take a right here into **Gum Cove** and explore the canals of this area.

**MILE 2.5:** At this point, you leave the more protected creek for the open waters of **Currituck Sound.** As you head north from here, stay close to the shore on your right.

**MILE 4.0:** You will paddle past a residential area the entire length of this portion of the Outer Banks.

**MILE 5.0:** You will be opposite the town of Duck. If you hug the coast you will see lots of ducks and other wading birds. There are also numerous shops and restaurants you can take out at if you wish.

**MILE 5.5:** The boat ramp at **Duck Landing** could be a takeout if you want to shuttle back to the launch site, or if you just want to get something to eat. Otherwise, turn around and retrace your route back to the launch site.

# Attack Swans

This area is home to a pair of mute swans that were left behind when a homeowner moved away. They are extremely territorial, so be cautious. They have been know to fly directly at kayakers to scare them away—it works. It is very intimidating to be rushed by a bird who is bigger than you, and whose head and beak come up to the top of your head. It is usually the male who charges, and he has been known to bite. One woman was so frightened that she fell out of her boat and swam to shore, abandoning her boat. When we went to retrieve the boat, there were the swans guarding the kayak. We had to use a stick to keep them at bay while we grabbed the boat and ran. If you spot these birds, keep your distance.

## Where to Eat & Where to Stay

**RESTAURANTS**  *Johns Drive-In*, located at milepost 4½ on NC–12 (252–261–2916), is billed as the "home of the planet's best milk shakes ." There are people who drive for two hours just to get one. The burgers are perfect, but do try a tuna or trout sandwich. Open May through October; closed on Wednesdays. Be prepared to wait.  **LODGING**  There are plenty of motels in the area. The *Holiday Inn Express* (800–836–2753) is 4 miles east of the launch site on U.S. 158 at milepost 4½. Open year-round.  **CAMPING**  *Outer Banks International Hostel* (252–261–2294) has a campground and rooms for rent. It's located on West Kitty Hawk Road, about 2 miles from the launch site.

# Route 5:

■■ ■■ ■ ■■ ■■ ■■ ■■ ■■ ■■ ■ ■■ ➤

## Kitty Hawk Woods Preserve

A local secret for years, Kitty Hawk Woods is one of five best maritime forests in the world. What makes it special is that plants and animals you would usually find in upland communities exist less than a quarter mile from the Atlantic Ocean. Protected from wind and weather, this creek is home to numerous types of wildlife, including white-tailed deer, otters, nutrias, and reptiles—lots of reptiles. The creek meanders through maritime shrub swamp, forest, sedge, and salt marsh habitat. Each zone has different plants and animals.

This 4-mile stretch of channel is known as Jean Guite Creek, High Bridge Creek, or Ginguite Creek, depending on whom you ask. Back in the 1800s, when the Outer Banks boasted a thriving lumber business, Jean Guite Creek served as a protected waterway on which log-carrying barges were towed. This 600-acre preserve is now comanaged by the Town of Kitty Hawk and the North Carolina Coastal Reserve.

The channel, widened but left relatively untouched, is perfect for a short trip, a full-day paddle, or as part of a multinight excursion. Although I describe a straight route, take time to explore the side creeks and coves that branch off from the main creek. They all end a short distance from the main course, so you can't get lost.

**TRIP HIGHLIGHTS:** Protected from wind, peaceful, and filled with wildlife, this is where you can find the only wooden covered bridge in eastern North Carolina.

**TRIP RATING:**   Beginner to intermediate.

**TRIP DURATION:**   Three hours to a full day; 8.5 miles, with an option for shortening the trip.

**NAVIGATION AIDS:**   ADC Outer Banks Visitors Map (the best map for the area—to order call 703–750–0510); NOAA chart #12205.

**TIDAL INFORMATION:**   Wind, not the moon, affects the water level here. With an east wind the water will be lower than with a west wind. The only time I've found it impassable is when the wind blew northeast, 25 to 35 miles per hour, for more than two days. With a strong west wind (greater than 20 miles per hour) you will be able to access some of the shallower side creeks that are impassable most of the time.

**CAUTIONS:**   If you are at all squeamish about snakes, wait for cold weather to travel this creek. This is a prime habitat for the water moccasin (a venomous snake) and other harmless ones. Hundreds of people use this creek yearly and no snakebites have ever been reported. To avoid problems, just remember a few basic rules: 1) Never throw anything at a snake or splash it. 2) A snake in the water always has the right of way. 3) Stay out of the bushes on the side of the creek, where many snakes like to curl up in the branches.

**TRIP PLANNING:**   Kitty Hawk Woods is open for day use only. I've found the best time of day for wildlife viewing is during mid-morning or in the evening. This route is accessible year-round. It is one of the few places you can paddle on the Outer Banks during high winds. The only time it may be difficult is if the wind has been blowing hard (25 knots or higher) from the northeast for several days. Wind like this will tend to blow the water out of the creek, making it difficult to paddle in the shallow water.

**LAUNCH SITE:**   The launch site is located at milepost ¼ on U.S. 158. The mile markers on the Outer Banks start at mile marker "0" at the Wright Memorial Bridge in Kitty Hawk and run south to mile marker 24 in Nags Head. Driving from the bridge, heading south, turn right into the parking lot of Kitty Hawk Kayaks, which is located between Coastal Chevrolet and the Flag Store. This store is open only during the summer season, but you can park there all year for no fee. Be sure to ask for permission first. Park in front and carry your kayak around back to the launch site. A portable toilet is available from April to November, otherwise you will need to drive south for another mile to the mall.

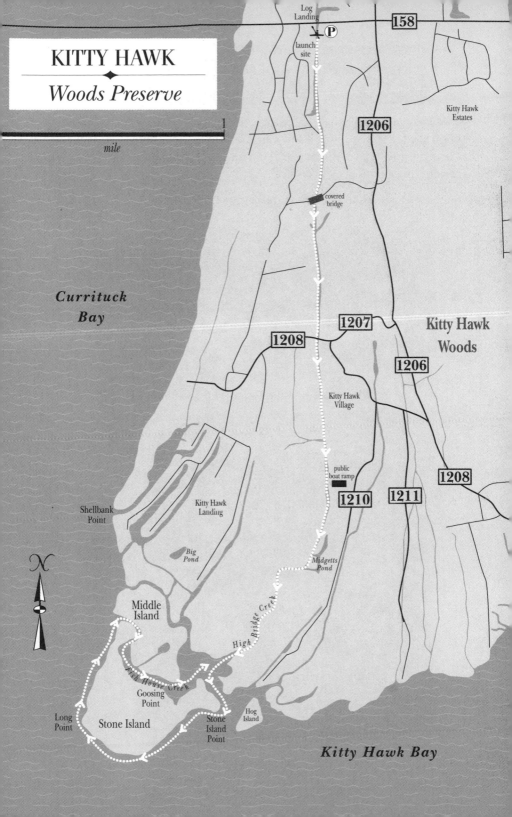

# KITTY HAWK
◆
## Woods Preserve

1 mile

**Log Landing**

**158**

launch site

**1206**

Kitty Hawk Estates

covered bridge

*Currituck Bay*

**1207**

**Kitty Hawk Woods**

**1208**

**1206**

Kitty Hawk Village

**1208**

public boat ramp

**1210**

**1211**

**1208**

Shellbank Point

Kitty Hawk Landing

*Big Pond*

*Midgetts Pond*

N

*High Bridge Creek*

Middle Island

*Fish House Creek*

Goosing Point

Stone Island Point

Hog Island

Long Point

Stone Island

*Kitty Hawk Bay*

**START:** From the ramp at the launch site, paddle south on **Jean Guite (High Bridge) Creek.** Just a few yards south of the launch site, you can take a right into a small cove. It dead-ends very shortly, but is a good spot for wildlife watching.

*MILE 0.75:* A massive **wooden bridge** spans the creek. This "Bridge to Nowhere," as it is called, is at the site of a failed housing development. This is a good place for spotting cottonmouth snakes. Look for them on the bank to the south of the bridge. Just south of here is where I've seen white-tailed deer along the side of the creek.

*MILE 2.0:* There are portable toilets at the **public boat ramp.** *Note:* This is a very busy boat launch during the summer months. The local fishermen launch from here to head out toward Kitty Hawk Bay.

*MILE 2.5:* The canal takes a turn to the right after you pass **Midgetts Pond.** Keep an eye out for boats making this turn. Keep to the right.

*MILE 3.0:* The canal widens as it merges with Fish House Creek. At this point, you may turn around and return along the same route, shortening the trip to 6 miles. Otherwise, turn left and paddle southeast between two marsh islands into **Kitty Hawk Bay.**

*MILE 3.25:* Turn right (southwest) around **Stone Island Point.**

*MILE 3.75:* You will be at the southernmost point of Stone Island. If you look south, you will see Colington Island. Follow the island's shoreline as it curves northwest toward **Long Point.**

*MILE 4.5:* Turn right into **Fish House Creek.** This is a good area for bird-watching, fishing, or crabbing. Follow the creek as it winds its way between Stone Island and **Middle Island.**

*MILE 5.25:* Fish House Creek widens just before you head back into Jean Guite (High Bridge) Creek. Paddle northeast into the creek, then follow it 3 miles to the takeout.

## Where to Eat & Where to Stay

**RESTAURANTS** There are many places to eat within a mile of the launch site. A favorite is *Southern Bean Coffee Shop* (252–261–5282), located in the Market Place shops on U.S. 158. They make great coffee, muffins, bagels, and vegetarian sandwiches. **LODGING** There are numerous places to stay in the immediate area. Contact the *Dare County Tourist Bureau* (252–473–2138) for a complete list. **CAMPING** *Outer Banks Hostel* (252–261–2294) is open year-round; rates start at $15. *Colington Park Campground* (252–441–5468) is one of the few places in the area where you can paddle up and camp. Rates are $14 for two people. Open year-round.

# Nutrias

What do you get when you cross a beaver with a rat? You'd probably get a nutria. Brought to the United States in 1899 from South America, nutrias are large aquatic rodents. They were introduced as a source of fur for garments. Nutrias, which weigh an average of 15 pounds, are larger than muskrats, and easier to breed. Their outer layer of hair is long and coarse but the underlayer is soft and thick.

Legend has it that they were penned on the ground and, as any self-respecting rodent would, they soon dug out. Nutrias may have up to five litters per year, so they did not take long to establish themselves in the wild. Although mainly vegetarian, they eat most anything, and they compete with our native species of muskrat and otter.

Nutrias live along riverbanks and in swamps and can cause extensive erosion damage by burrowing into the riverbanks. They resemble the otter when swimming, and are quite common along the North Carolina coast. Look for them in the marshes and creeks.

# Route 6:

‒ ‒ ‒ ‒ ‒ ‒ ‒ ‒ ‒ ‒ ‒ ➤

## *Colington Island*

**C**olington Island actually consists of two islands, Big Colington Island and Little Colington Island. Two bridges span the waterways that separate the two. If you were to be blindfolded and dropped off here, I doubt you would guess you were at the seashore. The land is surprisingly high, with steep, irregular hills on which grow pine, holly, dogwood, and oak. These hills are thickly wooded and are separated by low, swampy land.

Colington Island is very paddler friendly. The many creeks, marshes, and canals that wind through and around the islands are perfectly suited for an hour or a day's paddle. There are several campgrounds that you can paddle up to, and a great seafood restaurant. Many homes are built on the canals that crisscross the island. One of the best things about paddling Colington Island is that no matter which direction the wind is blowing, you can find a calm side to explore.

**TRIP HIGHLIGHTS:** Beautiful salt marsh, paddle-up camping, great crabbing.

**TRIP RATING:** Beginner.

**TRIP DURATION:** Three hours to all day; 7 miles.

**NAVIGATION AIDS:** ADC Map of the Outer Banks.

**TIDAL INFORMATION:** No direct tidal influence. Wind direction and speed will be the deciding factors.

**CAUTIONS:** Keep an eye out for boat traffic during the busy summer months.

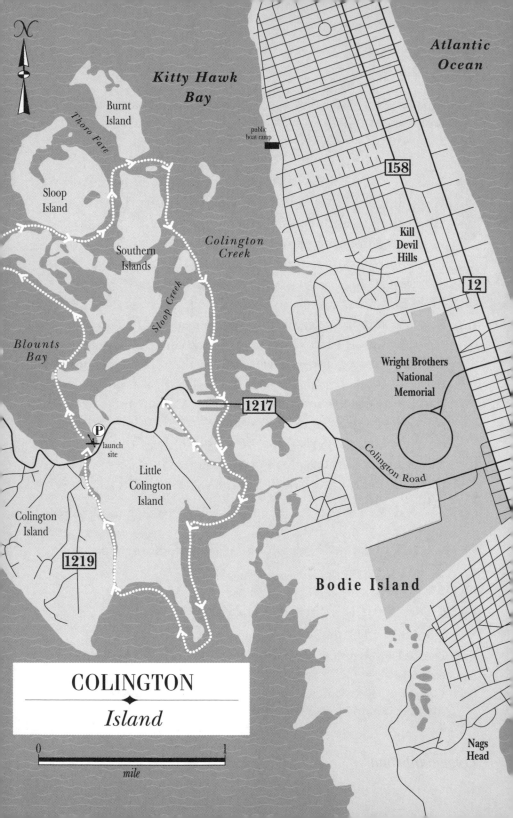

**N**

*Kitty Hawk Bay*

**Atlantic Ocean**

Burnt Island

*Thoro Fare*

public boat ramp

158

Sloop Island

Southern Islands

*Colington Creek*

*Sloop Creek*

Kill Devil Hills

12

*Blounts Bay*

Wright Brothers National Memorial

1217

P

launch site

Little Colington Island

*Colington Road*

Colington Island

1219

**Bodie Island**

**COLINGTON**

*Island*

Nags Head

0                    mile                    1

**TRIP PLANNING:** This is a good route for a day trip; if you wish to extend it, you can paddle across Kitty Hawk Bay to Jean Guite (High Bridge) Creek.

**LAUNCH SITE:** From U.S. 158 turn onto Colington Road, just before the Wright Brothers Memorial if you are heading north, and continue for 3 miles. Just after the second little bridge, you will see a parking area on your right. You can park here and put in directly in front of your vehicle.

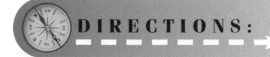

**DIRECTIONS:**

**START:** From the launch site head north in **Blounts Bay.** Keep on the south side of the waterway. Directly ahead of you will be the first of the Southern Islands.

**MILE 1.0:** Colington Island shoreline, across the bay on your left, will start to curve to the west. Follow the shoreline around the point, then turn right and head east between two islands, keeping **Sloop Island** to your left.

**MILE 2.0:** Follow the creek north for 0.25 mile, turning to your right around the tip of the island. You will pass **Thoro Fare** and **Burnt Island** on your left. Keep turning right until you are heading south in **Colington Creek.**

**MILE 3.0:** You will pass a small island on your right. Behind it is **Sloop Creek,** which leads back to Blounts Bay. You can turn here if you wish to take a shortcut back to the launch, otherwise keep heading south along Colington Creek.

**MILE 4.0:** Pass under the **Colington Road bridge** (NC–1217).

**MILE 4.25:** A canal on the right leads to the Oyster House Cafe, a nice spot for lunch. The canal is 0.25 mile long.

**MILE 5.5:** As you round the southernmost point of the route, continue turning right, keeping the shoreline on your right.

**MILE 6.0:** Take a right into the creek here and paddle 1 mile back to the launch site.

*Colington Island*

# Mile Markers

If you have never been to the Outer Banks before, the mile marker system may confuse you. After crossing the Wright Memorial Bridge the miles start ticking off as soon as you land on the Outer Banks side, starting with 0 in Kitty Hawk and ending at 16 in South Nags Head. The green mile markers are found on both the beach road and U.S. 158. Posted every mile, I've yet to see them all because they keep disappearing. It's hard to get lost even if you have trouble finding the mile markers, though. Just remember there are only two roads that parallel the Outer Banks: Virginia Dare Highway (the beach road) and U.S. 158 (known as the bypass).

## Where to Eat & Where to Stay

**RESTAURANTS** You can paddle up to the *Oyster Bar* (252–480–1400) at 1469 Colington Road, Kill Devil Hills. The *Colington Cafe* (252–480–1123) is one of my favorite restaurants on the entire coast. Stuck back into the woods of Colington, the owners turned a wonderful little cottage into a wonderful restaurant. Make reservations; I've never seen the place without a line. **LODGING** The *Ramada Inn* (252–441–2151 or 800–635–1824), on the beach in Kill Devil Hills, is very paddler friendly. **CAMPING** *Joe & Kay's* (252–441–5468) and *Colington Park Campground* (252–441–6128) are both on Colington Road, about 1 mile apart. You can paddle up to both of them.

# Route 7:

▬▬ ▬▬ ▬▬ ▬▬ ▬▬ ▬▬ ▬▬ ▬▬ ▬▬ ▬▬ ➤

## Nags Head Woods and Jockey's Ridge

**Y**ou can't miss Jockey's Ridge. This huge sand dune is the tallest on the East Coast. Surrounded by Jockey's Ridge State Park, Jockey's Ridge is between 110 and 140 feet tall, depending on the winds and weather. It's always on the move. The prevailing winds move the ridge from southwest to northeast and back again. It's great fun to climb the hill and then either run or roll down. During the winter months, when this area gets a rare dusting of snow, you'll find locals skimming down the slope on body boards and anything else that slides.

**TRIP HIGHLIGHTS:** Paddling past Jockey's Ridge State Park; some of the best sunsets; windsurfers flitting about like so many brightly-colored butterflies.

**TRIP RATING:** Intermediate.

**TRIP DURATION:** Five to six hours; 12 miles.

**NAVIGATION AIDS:** ADC Map of the Outer Banks.

**TIDAL INFORMATION:** No direct tidal influence.

**CAUTIONS:** This route can be very shallow in a northeast wind. Plan your trip on a light wind day or a day with a west wind.

**TRIP PLANNING:** This is a good route to plan close to sunset. People by the hundreds climb to the top of the ridge to watch the sunset from the highest point of land on the Outer Banks.

**LAUNCH SITE:** There are two launch sites. The first one is located at milepost 16 on U.S. 158 in Nags Head, between Kitty Hawk Watersports and Windmill Point Restaurant, on the sound side. It is a Town of Nags Head public boat launch and it's just for nonmotorized vessels. This ramp is open twenty-four hours a day.

The second launch site is located directly behind Jockey's Ridge State Park on Soundside Road West. This parking area closes at dark, so make sure you are back by then, or plan on leaving your vehicle there overnight since they lock the gates at dusk.

# DIRECTIONS:

**START:** From the first launch site, turn right and head north, keeping the banks on your right.

**MILE 1.0:** Pass **Nags Head Golf Links** on your right.

**MILE 2.25:** Reach the old Nags Head Cove public access. *Caution:* Keep an eye out for boat traffic through the area.

**MILE 3.0:** The second launch site, at **Jockey's Ridge State Park,** will be on your right. The water can be very shallow here in northeast winds. If you want to climb Jockey's Ridge, you can pull your kayak up on the beach and explore.

**MILE 4.25:** Continue to follow the shoreline to the northwest, passing Nags Head Woods, a maritime forest.

**MILE 5.75:** Turn right (north), rounding Manns Point.

**MILE 6.0:** Paddle into the cove that leads into **Nags Head Woods Nature Preserve.** This is a good place to get out to take a break or hike the trails in the preserve. Follow the same route back to the launch site.

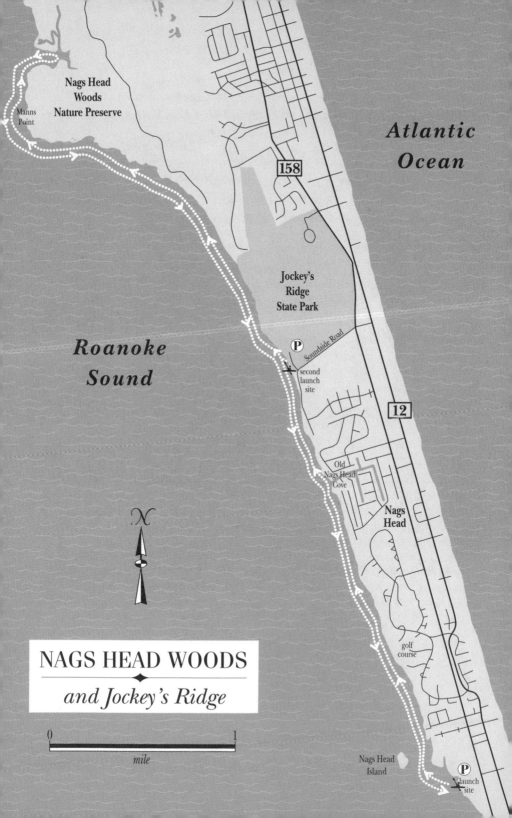

**Nags Head Woods Nature Preserve**

Manns Point

**Atlantic Ocean**

158

Jockey's Ridge State Park

**Roanoke Sound**

P

Soundside Road

second launch site

12

Old Nags Head Cove

**Nags Head**

golf course

## NAGS HEAD WOODS
### and Jockey's Ridge

0                    1
*mile*

Nags Head Island

P

launch site

# Otters

River otters are found throughout coastal North Carolina. Weighing between 10 and 30 pounds, an otter is 3 to 4 feet long from the tip of its nose to the end of its tail.

Although sea otters swim belly up and float high in the water due to their air-filled fur, river otters like to swim belly down, showing very little of their backs. They are capable of swimming at a rate of 7 miles an hour and can dive to depths of 180 feet.

Otters are very playful and are known for their social behavior. It's quite common to see them on the shores of the salt marsh, diving and chasing each other. You will often see a mother with several of her young. Look for them in inland creeks and along the shoreline on the sound side.

## Where to Eat & Where to Stay

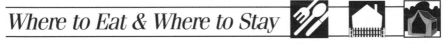

**RESTAURANTS**  *How Sweet It Is* (252–441–4485) is a great deli located directly across from Jockey's Ridge at Jockey's Ridge Crossing shopping center, milepost 13. Great sandwiches, veggie burgers, Boar's Head meats. *Bacu Grill* (252–480–1892) is located at the Outer Banks Mall, milepost 14.5. It serves Cuban specials and great seafood, including coconut shrimp and cracked conch. **LODGING**  *Islander Motel* (252–441–6229) is located on NC–12 at milepost 16 on the ocean. **CAMPING**  *Andy's Travel Park* (252–441–5251), at milepost 15 on U.S. 158, allows trailers and tent camping. It's the only campground on the strip and stays full during most of the warmer months.

# Route 8:

▬ ▬ ▬ ▬ ▬ ▬ ▬ ▬ ▬ ▬ ▬ ▬ ▬ ▬ ➤

## Pond Island to Headquarters Island

This section is the northernmost portion of the Cape Hatteras National Seashore. There are numerous access points, but I've pointed out the most convenient to use. This is a beautiful area comprising creeks and marsh. There is an abundance of bird life to see here, as well as some great fishing and crabbing. The islands in this section are dotted with old hunting shacks and rustic vacation cabins that the locals still use.

**TRIP HIGHLIGHTS:** Paddling in the beautiful Bodie Island salt marsh; lots of wading birds, ospreys, and other wildlife.

**TRIP RATING:** Beginner.

**TRIP DURATION:** Three to four hours; 4.5 miles.

**NAVIGATION AIDS:** ADC Map of the Outer Banks.

**TIDAL INFORMATION:** No direct tidal influence.

**CAUTIONS:** Waterfowl hunting is allowed. Contact the National Park Service (252–441–2111) to find out when duck season starts, and avoid the area during hunting season.

**TRIP PLANNING:** Plan around hunting season.

**LAUNCH SITE:** The launch site is located on Pond Island, U.S. 64/264, on the Manteo–Nags Head Causeway, directly across the street from the Oasis Restaurant. This is a Town of Nags Head facility with a rest room. Park in the lot and walk to the bulkheaded beach, just south of the little bridge. A dirt path leads to the kayak launch, which is the only place to put in. Do not launch off the riprap; it is unstable.

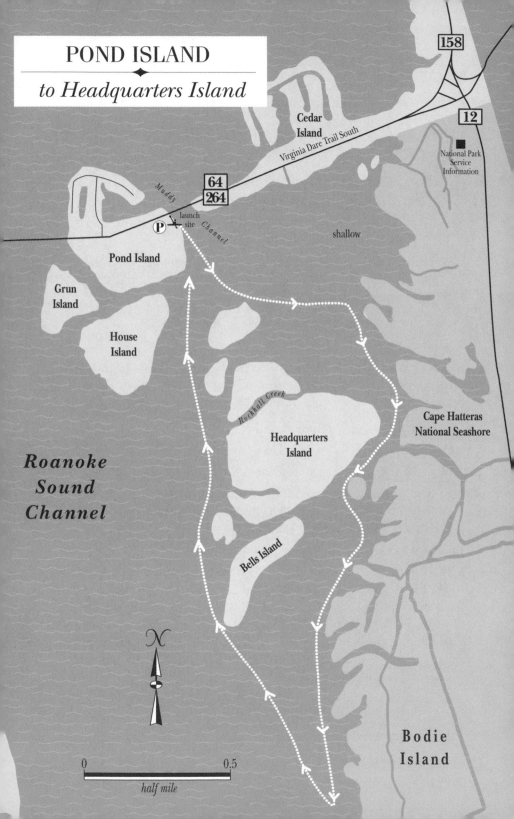

# DIRECTIONS:

**START:** From the launch, head south, angling east. Head toward the island you see straight ahead. Keep to the left of the island, staying fairly close to its shore.

**MILE 0.25:** Once you reach the island turn east and head for the shore on your left. Several small indentations along the shore harbor lots of wading birds.

**MILE 1.0:** A deeper cove winds back into the marsh where many birds can be found. I especially like to watch the ospreys dive into the water and fly off with a fish or snake between their talons.

Along the next mile are several openings into the marsh, which lead almost to NC–12 if the water is high enough. These narrow canals are the same ones used by the duck hunters in the fall. Crabs, shrimp, fish, oysters, clams, and mussels abound in this area.

**MILE 2.5:** To return to the launch area, turn right and head northwest. When you see the first island ahead of you **(Bells Island)** stay to the left, keeping the island on your right. This will take you past **Headquarters Island,** where there is a private hunting cabin. I daydream of one day having just such a place to just kick back, read, and relax.

**MILE 4.0:** Once you pass Headquarters Island, stay to the right of the island ahead of you **(House Island).** Continue north, toward the east side of Pond Island. The takeout is 0.75 mile north of Headquarters Island.

*Pond Island to Headquarters Island*

# The Salt Marsh

Known as the nurseries of the Atlantic, salt marshes are the meeting place between the ocean and the land. They extend hundreds of miles along the North Carolina coast.

While you are paddling in the salt marshes of North Carolina, take a close look at the plants that thrive in this harsh environment. Wax myrtle, marsh elder, seaside goldenrod, and yaupon have waxy, leathery leaves that can resist salt damage and retain moisture. Glasswort, sea blite, and other succulents can store water in leaf tissue, which helps them to withstand a high salt content without stress. Plants such as cordgrass and spike grass have the ability to secrete salt.

One of the most productive natural ecosystems in the world, a salt marsh can produce as much food as a wheat field. The plants in the marsh are the primary producers of food. When they die and decompose, rich nutrients are washed into the estuary by the rising and falling of the tides. These nutrients help to support plankton, which in turn is the base for the salt marsh food pyramid and is eaten by many of the animals that live there. The marsh is also an important source of seafood, such as oysters, clams, shrimp, scallops, and many types of fish.

## Where to Eat & Where to Stay

**RESTAURANTS** *Basnight's Lone Cedar Cafe* (252–441–5405) on U.S. 64/264 (Manteo–Nags Head Causeway), is one of several restaurants on the causeway that you can paddle up to. They serve seafood, burgers, and vegetarian dishes. Good food and a beautiful view. Open for lunch and dinner.
**LODGING** *Fin and Feather Motel* (252–441–5353 or 888–441–5353) is located on U.S. 64/264 right on the water. Your basic motel, but what a location.
**CAMPING** See Route 7, Nags Head and Jockey's Ridge.

# Route 9:

▬ ▬ ▬ ▬ ▬ ▬ ▬ ▬ ▬ ▬ ▬ ▬ ➤

## Roanoke Island:
## Shallowbag Bay to Broad Creek

I admit I'm a little bit biased when it comes to Roanoke Island. I've lived and paddled here for fifteen years. No matter what the weather or wind direction, you can always find a calm place to paddle. Explore the waterfront and the soft crab operations along the canals of downtown Manteo and Mother Vineyard. Take an evening paddle past the Lost Colony to see the nightly fireworks, which are a part of the outdoor drama. Wander the deserted beaches on the island's west side. Look for Civil War artifacts along the shoreline near Skyco on the southwest side, where 10,000 troops were stationed during the war. You can paddle from Wanchese Harbor on the southern end of the island, taking in the commercial fishing village and the surrounding salt marsh, and maybe take along a fishing pole to try your luck in some of the most fertile fishing ground on the Outer Banks.

**TRIP HIGHLIGHTS:**  Scenery, bird-watching, dolphins.

**TRIP RATING:**  Intermediate to advanced.

**TRIP DURATION:**  Four to five hours; 7 miles.

**NAVIGATION AIDS:**  ADC Map of the Outer Banks.

**TIDAL INFORMATION:**  Tidal influence is not a factor here.

**CAUTIONS:**  There can be heavy boat traffic in this area in the morning and early evening during the warmer months. Charter boats returning to the dock pass right by and can create large wakes. The public boat ramp is also heavily used during the

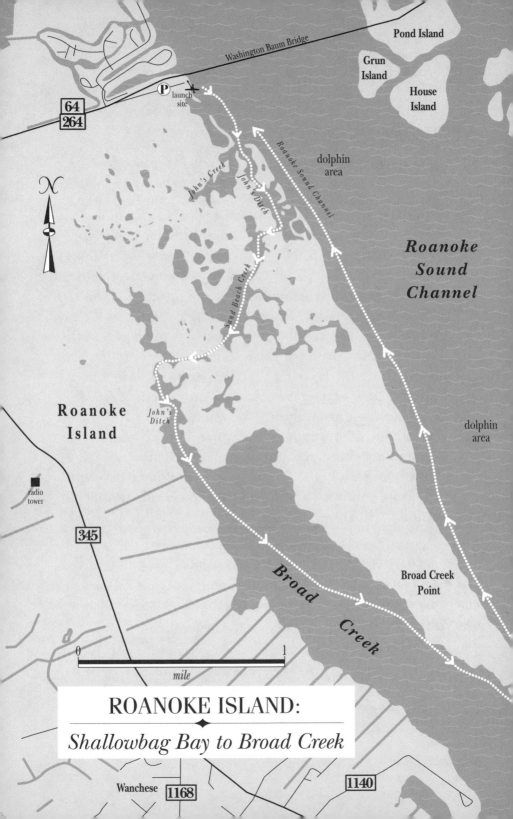

Pond Island

Grun Island

House Island

Washington Baum Bridge

64
264

P launch site

John's Creek

John's Ditch

Roanoke Sound Channel

dolphin area

N

Roanoke Sound Channel

Sand Beach Creek

Roanoke Island

John's Ditch

radio tower

345

dolphin area

Broad Creek Point

Broad Creek

0          1
mile

ROANOKE ISLAND:
Shallowbag Bay to Broad Creek

Wanchese  1168          1140

summer months. This area is also exposed and can prove difficult to paddle in if it is windy. Use caution if the wind is from the north at more than 20 knots.

**TRIP PLANNING:** In the summer this trip is best done in the morning or evening due to the heat.

**LAUNCH SITE:** From U.S. 64/264 in Nags Head, cross the Washington Baum Bridge onto Roanoke Island. Turn left at the stoplight and follow the side road back under the bridge to the parking area. The best place to put in is next to the boat ramp on the far left side, where there is a bulkhead with a small sand beach. This is the safest place to get your boat ready, as the ramps are very busy and quite slippery. There are rest rooms available and plenty of parking.

## DIRECTIONS:

**START:** From the put in turn south (right). Take care to swing wide so you are not right next to the boat ramp. This is a public ramp and is used heavily during the season. Follow the coast south for about 0.25 mile.

**MILE 0.25:** You will see a point of land directly ahead of you. Continue paddling south for 0.5 mile, staying to the right of this point. This area is the start of **John's Ditch.** It is a beautiful, easy-to-paddle creek through the salt marsh. There are some great fishing holes in here as well as lots of birds. It is easy to get confused and take the wrong turn if you lose track of where you are. I'm pretty sure no one has ever gotten completely lost, never to be seen again, but you don't want to be the first.

**MILE 0.75:** Follow **Sand Beach Creek** as it branches off to the right. If you look down the creek and can see for quite a ways, you will know you have the correct route. Continue along the creek as it bends toward your left (south). As you paddle along the main creek, you will pass two more openings in the marsh on your right, one every tenth of a mile or so. Don't take these; stay to your left.

**MILE 1.5:** You'll reach a tricky spot at a Y in the creek; you want to go toward the left. You will know you are on the right path if the main creek takes a sharp bend to the left directly after this. It should gradually get wider until it opens up into **Broad Creek**.

# Roanoke Island

Roanoke Island is only 7 miles from the beaches, but a world away. Surrounded by water and steeped in history, Roanoke Island is worth a day or two of your time off the water to explore fully.

Sir Walter Raleigh, a British subject who was fancied by the Queen, sought her help in a venture. He wanted to colonize the New World in order to establish British presence and to build a fort from which they could sail to attack Spanish ships. In 1584 a small band of Raleigh's men came ashore, liked what they found, and returned to England with two Native Americans to report what they had found. They named the land Virginia after Elizabeth, their virgin queen.

In the spring of 1585, the next group set sail. Their task was to look for gold and silver, establish a settlement, and build a fort; 107 soldiers were left to do this while the captain went south in search of ships to pirate and plunder. The 107 men, being unaccustomed to farming, were unable to sustain themselves and demanded the Indians feed them. This obviously caused some problems and the natives deserted them. Just when things seemed hopeless, Sir Francis Drake sailed into the harbor and gave them a ship full of supplies. The ship, however, was swept out to sea and they made a hard decision to abandon the fort and sail back with Drake to England.

Only days after they departed, the captain who had left them returned to find everything deserted. He left fifteen more men to guard the abandoned fort and he sailed back to England as well. These men were never found again. They were believed to be massacred by the natives their shipmates angered.

Back in England, a final group of colonists was preparing to depart. By now, Raleigh was running out of capital and had decided that this would be the last trip. In 1587, seventy-nine men, seventeen women, and eight children boarded the ships for their journey of several months. They had decided to head farther north, toward present day Jamestown, Virginia, but a quarrel erupted between the captain, Simon Fernando, and the new governor, John White, who were unceremoniously dumped off on Roanoke Island. When

Fernando left a month later to return to England, he invited White to go back for more supplies. White reluctantly agreed, leaving behind his daughter and her new baby, Virginia Dare, the first English child born in the New World. He gave them instructions to leave a written sign somewhere visible to let him know where they were headed if they had to leave.

England was now at war with Spain and the Queen would allow no vessels to leave. It was not until 1590, three years later, that White was finally able to procure a ship to return to Virginia. When he arrived, he found nothing except the word *Croatan* inscribed on a tree. He never saw his daughter or granddaughter again.

To this day, no one is really sure what happened to those colonists, now know as the "Lost Colony." You can visit the reconstructed Fort Raleigh on Route 64 on the north end of the

*(continued on next page)*

island. During the summer months, an outdoor play that tells the story of this ill-fated group is presented each night. This play has been running since 1937 and combines dance, drama, and music. Next door to Fort Raleigh National Historic Site is the Elizabethan Gardens. The Garden Club of North Carolina created these gardens as a memorial to the first colonists. Take a few hours to wander the tree-shaded paths, which are surrounded by breathtaking flowers and plants.

The Elizabeth II Maritime Historic Site is another stop worth making. Located on the waterfront in downtown Manteo, you can paddle right by it. This 69-foot square-rigged sailing ship was built as a representation of one of the vessels Sir Walter Raleigh's colonists sailed to the New World. The visitor center and entrance to the ship are located at the end of Highway 400, across a bridge form the Manteo waterfront. A working vessel, the best time to visit is during the summer months when a living-history crew re-creates a day aboard the *Elizabeth II* in the 1500s.

*MILE 2.0:* Follow Broad Creek as it opens up, staying close to the left bank, and head east. Take time to poke into the little creeks and coves that branch off from it. I've seen lots of birds and snakes here. The snakes should not bother you if you keep your distance. They are interesting to watch as they swim and feed along the banks of the marsh. Look for clams, oysters, and shrimp, too. Toward the middle of Broad Creek, it is not uncommon to see dolphins, but the majority of them stay in Roanoke Sound.

*MILE 3.5:* You'll reach the point of land where Broad Creek and Roanoke Sound merge. At this point you may turn around and retrace your path up John's Ditch or round the point and head north, back to the put in. If you wish to go a bit farther, you could head south 1 mile to Wanchese Harbor and then return.

*Caution:* Roanoke Sound is the main channel for the fishing fleet, which leaves from Pirates Cove Marina. The channel comes very close to the shoreline. These boats may be more than 60 feet long, and they do create big wakes. This is usually just a problem when the boats are returning in the afternoon, around 4:30 P.M. Those who are not comfortable paddling in a wake zone will want to return along John's Ditch.

**MILE 4.0:** As you paddle north, keep a lookout for dolphins. They are very common in this area during the warmer months. They love kayaks and come very close, but the Marine Mammal Protection Act prohibits feeding, swimming with, or in any way harassing these marine mammals. Just take pictures and memories.

This area is also one of my favorites for short paddles to one of the pretty beaches along this stretch. You can bring a picnic lunch, paddle a mile or so, and spend all day. You can even put up a tent on one of the higher patches of land here. Remember to be discreet with your camping and follow no-impact camping rules. Set up camp close to dark, out of sight of the water. Nighttime paddling during the full moon is fantastic in this area.

# Where to Eat & Where to Stay

**RESTAURANTS** *Hurricane Mo's* (252–473–2266) is located at Pirates Cove Marina just yards north of the put in. You can paddle up or drive your vehicle. They have a raw bar, outside deck, and great seafood. Open for lunch and dinner during the season. *Note:* Restaurants on Roanoke Island can serve only wine and beer, but they do allow brown-bagging (you bring your own liquor). **LODGING** There are several reasonable motels within 2 miles of this route. The *Island Motel and Guest House* (252–473–2434) is very kayaker friendly. Owner Sam Moore even has a few kayaks to rent if you need an extra. *Duke of Dare Motor Lodge* (252–473–2175) offers a pool, nice rooms, and muffins for breakfast. **CAMPING** *Cypress Cove Campground* (252–473–5231) is located 1 mile from the put in. This wooded, year-round campground even has a stocked fishing pond and a short nature trail. Rates are $17 a night.

# Route 10:

■ ■ ■ ■ ■ ■ ■ ■ ■ ■ ■ ■ ■ ➤

## Roanoke Island:
## Wanchese Harbor to Hog Island

**W**anchese, located on the southern end of Roanoke Island, is a real fishing village. Drive down any of its streets and you'll most likely see a boat or fishing nets in the yards. As many as fifty large commercial fishing vessels fill the harbor, and fish-packing plants as well as seafood stores line the waterfront. Many of the residents of this individualist village still earn their living from the sea.

Once you leave Wanchese Harbor, the southern end of Roanoke Island is inhabited only by wildlife. There are many great fishing holes in its numerous coves and creeks. I recommend spending a day poking around, fishing, or just relaxing.

**TRIP HIGHLIGHTS:** Beautiful marshes, great bird-watching, and the active fishing harbor of Wanchese.

**TRIP RATING:** Intermediate to advanced.

**TRIP DURATION:** Four to five hours; 8.25 miles.

**NAVIGATION AIDS:** ADC Map of the Outer Banks; USGS Map NC0786, Wanchese, North Carolina, 1:24,000 scale.

**TIDAL INFORMATION:** No direct tidal influence.

**CAUTIONS:** This is a very busy harbor; watch out for boat traffic. Large fishing trawlers dock at the wharf and can create quite a wake.

**TRIP PLANNING:** The best time of day to start this trip is midmorning. Try to return before 5:00 P.M., since the fishing boats are returning at this time. Although there is boat traffic all day, this will keep you out of the harbor during the busiest time.

**LAUNCH SITE:** From Nags Head, follow U.S. 64/264 into Roanoke Island. Cross the Washington Baum Bridge and go 1.25 miles to a left turn onto Route 345 at the second stoplight. Follow Route 345 south for 4 miles. Turn left into the parking lot in front of Fisherman's Wharf Restaurant. Once in the parking lot, you will see the dock where you can launch from on your left. There is a public boat ramp as well, but it is very slippery, so use extreme caution.

## DIRECTIONS:

*START:* From the launch site, turn right (south). Stay clear of the rusted, half-sunken fishing boats on your right. Paddle for a short distance until you reach the mouth of the harbor.

*MILE 0.25:* Turn right and paddle for 1.25 miles until you see a large opening on your right.

*MILE 1.5:* This **cut through** will bring you into the prettiest part of the marsh and some good fishing or crabbing spots. You'll see terns, pelicans, herons, egrets, and dolphins. Paddle south toward **Hog Island.**

*MILE 2.0:* Continue south for 0.75 mile until you reach the end of Hog Island. At this time you may wish to turn around and slowly make your way back.

*MILE 2.75:* As you reach the southernmost point of Hog Island, you will turn right between Hog Island on your right and **Smith Island** on your left. Paddle to the northwest around the point and then follow the shoreline.

*MILE 4.0:* At the northern end of Hog Island, turn around and start to retrace your route.

*MILE 5.0:* As you reach this point, keep to the right of the shoreline, so you will pass to the south of Smith Island.

*MILE 5.25:* As you reach the southern end of Smith Island, turn left and head north.

*MILE 6.5:* Retrace your route through the cut through, and continue paddling north toward the harbor.

*MILE 8.0:* Turn into Wanchese Harbor, keeping to the left of the channel. Stay out of the main boat channel to avoid any boat traffic.

*Roanoke Island: Wanchese Harbor to Hog Island*

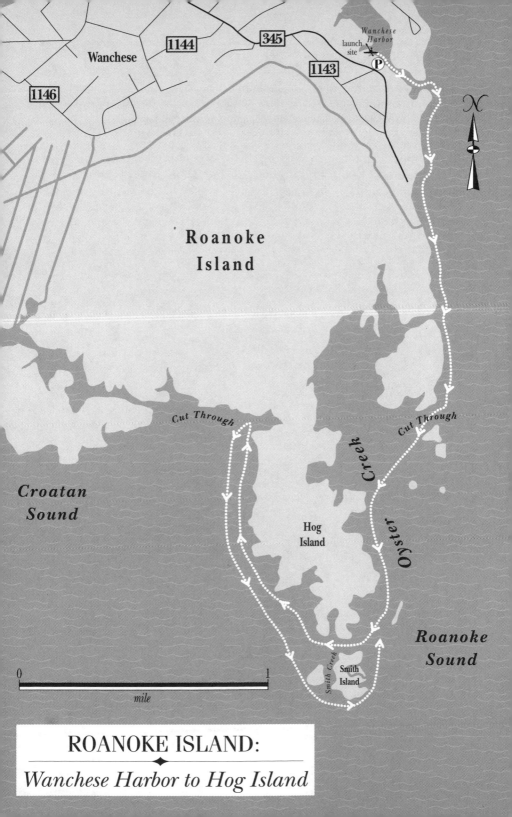

# ROANOKE ISLAND:
*Wanchese Harbor to Hog Island*

# Where to Eat & Where to Stay

**RESTAURANTS**   *Fisherman's Wharf Restaurant* (252–473–5205), located right on the docks, is a local family restaurant that serves some of the freshest seafood around. The restaurant is next to the fish-packing operation where the trawlers return from fishing offshore. *Queen Anne's Revenge* (252–473–5466), on Old Wharf Road in Wanchese, serves great seafood. It's named after one of Blackbeard's pirate ships, which sailed the local waters in the early 1700s. **LODGING**   *Island House of Wanchese Bed and Breakfast* (252–473–5619) is a quaint B&B next to Queen Anne's Revenge. It offers complimentary bikes and a hot tub for guests.   **CAMPING**   *Cypress Cove Campground* (252–473–5231), U.S. 64 in Manteo, right before the County Kitchen restaurant, also rents cabins that sleep one to six people.

# Dolphins

Spend any time at all on the coastal waters of North Carolina, and you will most likely come face to face with one of the most loved marine mammals, the Atlantic bottlenose dolphin. Dolphins live in the sounds and ocean of North Carolina. They belong to the whale family and, unlike fish, must come to the surface to breathe. They sleep under the water, putting themselves into a zombielike state by turning off half their brain. Each side rests for two hours every day. The females give birth to their young underwater and the baby is pushed to the surface by the "midwives" for its first breath.

Dolphins swim in pods for protection, feeding, sleeping, and fun. If you watch a group of dolphins for a few days, you will be able to pick out the same animals every day. The mothers with children like to stay in the center of the pod for protection. The older males tend to surround the females, and the adolescents—like children everywhere—stay on the outskirts of the pod where they can explore, play, and generally mess around.

Many people confuse dolphins with porpoises. A dolphin has a longer snout and is much bigger than a porpoise, growing up to 10 feet long and weighing up to 600 pounds. They can live for fifty years.

There is nothing like being in a kayak among a pod of dolphins. They will swim right up to your boat and eye you, or leap and splash in the water. Keep in mind that the Marine Mammal Protection Act prohibits swimming with dolphins, chasing them, or in any way harassing them.

# Route 11:

------------- ➤

## *Roanoke Island: West Side*

**I**t's hard to imagine that you are exploring an inhabited
island when you paddle on the west side of Roanoke Island.
While the north end of the island is marked by high
ground and quite a few homes, the southern and western
sides are relatively low, marshy, and secluded. Homes are
few and the beaches are deserted and covered with white
sand. You can easily spend a whole day beach hopping. I've
spent days and days exploring every inch of the west side,
combing the beach for that special find.

This area was the site of a large battle during the Civil
War. In 1862, most of the Outer Banks were in the
possession of the United States forces; Roanoke Island and
all the upper sounds were held by the Confederacy. A major
battle was imminent over the control of this island and its
crucial position. On February 7, 1862, the Burnside
expedition, with more than eighty vessels and a land force
of troops, was making plans for an attack. The waters of
Croatan Sound and the beaches of Ashby Harbor (now
Skyco) on the west side were the target. At 10:30 the first
shots were fired by the Confederate gunboats at the shore
batteries and the U.S. Forces' "Mosquito Fleet" of nine
oddly matched vessels. By midnight, 7,500 Federal troops
were bivouacked at Ashby Harbor, ready for a full-scale
attack at dawn. The surrounding marshes and the swampy
terrain slowed down the Federal forces, but they succeeded
in capturing the island along with 2,675 Confederate troops.

You can still find traces of this battle and the forts that
used to stand here. If you scuba dive or snorkel, you will

find a large collection of cannonballs, bottles, and other artifacts. I once put what I thought was a rock in the pocket of my vest for extra weight. My son, who liked to break rocks with hammers, smacked it a few times and discovered a cannonball fuse with the date 1861 on it. I've also found many Indian artifacts such as pieces of clay pipes and arrowheads on this side of the island. Whatever your interest is, spend a few hours exploring the shoreline of this unusual island.

**TRIP HIGHLIGHTS:** Secluded beaches, calm water, and the possibility of finding lots of good "stuff."

**TRIP RATING:** Beginner to advanced, depending on weather and wind conditions.

**TRIP DURATION:** Two to four hours; 3.5 miles, with additional 2-mile option.

**TIDAL INFORMATION:** No tidal influence other than wind tides.

**CAUTIONS:** Fishing nets are common here. Watch for lines of poles or narrow posts set out into the sound 50 to 100 yards from the shore. Pound nets are strung along these poles and left up to catch fish as they swim through. These nets can also snag rudders. Ensure that no nets are strung out before you go between the poles.

**TRIP PLANNING:** The best time to take this trip is when the wind is from the east or northeast. This way you will get some protection from the island. If the wind is coming from the south or northwest, be cautious of waves. They can push you onto the beach and make paddling less than enjoyable.

**LAUNCH SITE:** Take U.S. 64/264 from Nags Head into Manteo. In front of the Chesley Mall (Food-a-rama, Dollar General) take a left onto Bowsertown Road. Follow this for 0.25 mile until it ends in front of the old town refuse site. Turn left onto California Street; you will see the canal immediately on your right. Continue down California Street for a few yards and turn right into the public boat ramp parking lot. You may unload your boat next to the ramp before parking your vehicle. Once privately owned, this ramp was only recently opened to the public.

*Roanoke Island: West Side*

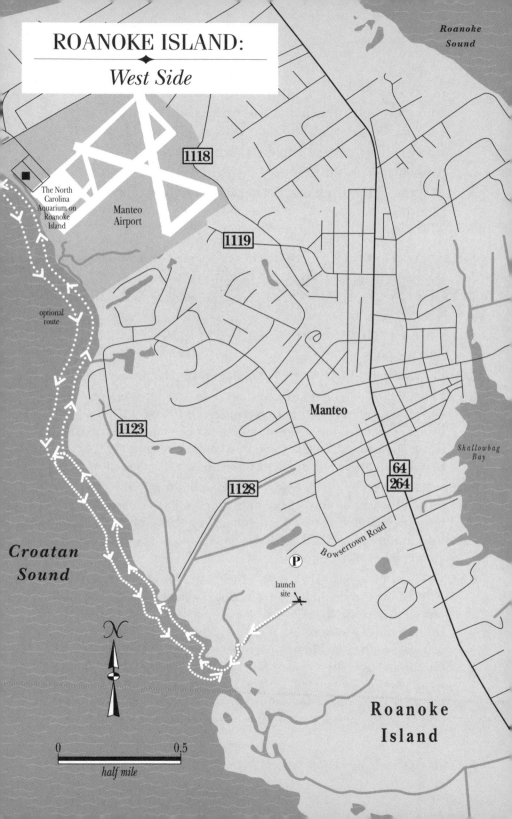

# ROANOKE ISLAND:
## West Side

**1118**

**1119**

The North
Carolina
Aquarium on
Roanoke
Island

Manteo
Airport

*Roanoke
Sound*

optional
route

**1123**

**1128**

Manteo

*Shallowbag
Bay*

**64**
**264**

*Croatan
Sound*

Bowsertown Road

P

launch
site

N

0                    0.5
*half mile*

**Roanoke
Island**

**START:** From the launch site, follow the canal for 0.25 mile. As you paddle down the canal, you will notice on your right the remains of the town refuse dump. No longer in operation, you will nonetheless still see quite a bit of trash around. I try to pick up as much as I can; every little bit helps.

**MILE 0.25:** The canal turns to the left and makes its way out to the sound. Keep to your right to reach the open water of **Croatan Sound.** You will notice several creeks off to your left. These are wonderful little side trips that you may want to follow. I've seen so much wildlife here: crabs, oysters, mussels, fish, snakes, and lots of birds. I've even seen raccoons and nutrias feeding along the marsh's edge.

**MILE 0.5:** Once you reach the open sound, turn right (north). Follow the shoreline for 0.5 mile and you will soon see another canal on your right. You may explore this if you wish; it has several old docks along it and some nice side creeks. Take the creeks that branch off to your right. The one that goes left is very shallow and gets quite narrow. *Side trip:* If you wish to see the new bridge being built to the mainland, turn left when you reach the sound. The bridge, when completed in 2002, will be the longest in North Carolina, spanning 7 miles. This is also the route to follow if you wish to explore **Skyco** (old Ashbee Harbor), the location of the Civil War battle.

**MILE 1.0:** Just past the canal is one of my favorite beaches; it has an old live oak tree on it. I usually continue a few yards more before I land. Although the land is privately owned, camping is allowed on these beaches, which are accessible only by boat. Be sure to camp above the high tide mark, be discreet in your selection of sites, and leave no trace.

From here the shoreline continues in a series of scalloped beaches in between patches of marsh.

**MILE 1.75:** The shoreline bends to the right. To return to the launch site, turn around and head south, keeping the shoreline on your left. After 1.75 miles you will pass the first canal on your left. Paddle another 0.5 mile and turn left into the exit canal.

**OTHER OPTIONS:** You can continue to follow the shoreline north 1.25 miles to the **North Carolina Aquarium.** Recently renovated, it was reopened in May 2000. The outstanding exhibits include a touch tank, a

*Roanoke Island: West Side*

shark tank, and extensive information on the coastal habitat. It's well worth the visit.

## Where to Eat & Where to Stay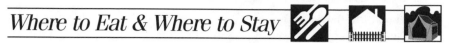

See Route 10, Roanoke Island. Do explore the many restaurants located in downtown Manteo, on the waterfront.

# Route 12:

■ ■ ■ ■ ■ ■ ■ ■ ■ ■ ■ ■ ━━▶

## Durant Island

**T**his beautiful island, just twenty minutes from the main beaches of Nags Head, is a true local secret. You won't find it in any guidebook, and most people don't even know it is here. It's a relatively low island with some higher areas on the north side. It is privately owned, but I have never been able to find out who the owners are. The U.S. Fish and Wildlife Service once used part of the island to house the red wolf. The experiment did not work: All the wolves left and swam to the mainland, where they still exist today.

There are some old fish camps on the northeast shore, which are used during different times of the year by the owners and friends. The fishing is pretty good in summer and fall, especially during rockfish season. (If you've never had rockfish, also called striped bass, you are surely missing something great. It has a mild flavor that reminds me of lobster.) There is an old shipwreck just west of Haulover Point. This would be a good place to fish, snorkel, or even scuba dive. It's very shallow, only a few feet.

If swimming or fishing is not for you, there are plenty of peaceful paddling areas to find. As you paddle on the west side, keep an eye out for the resident bald eagles. A pair of them nests just across the Alligator River and they are fairly easy to spot flying and hunting.

**TRIP HIGHLIGHTS:** Secluded beaches and high ground make this a perfect destination for a day or overnight trip.

**TRIP RATING:** Intermediate to advanced.

**TRIP DURATION:** Full day; 17.5 miles.

**TIDAL INFORMATION:** No tidal influence, other than wind tides.

**CAUTIONS:** This island is very secluded and not visited very much. Make sure you have the proper paddling skills. Pack everything you'll need. There are no facilities on the island, so bring plenty of water and food. Always watch the weather. Although there is some high ground to get to in the event of a storm, the entire island is prone to flooding and very secluded, so use caution when planning your trip.

**TRIP PLANNING:** This is a long paddle through open areas, so plan your trip carefully. If the wind is blowing hard you will have rough water at some point, no matter what direction you paddle. If you are traveling to Durant Island during the summer months, make sure you pack insect repellent. The flies can be bothersome. I like to visit here during the cooler months.

**LAUNCH SITE:** From Roanoke Island, take U.S. 64/264 across the William B. Ulmstead Bridge. Take your first right onto SR–1113, Mashoes Road. Follow Mashoes Road for 1.5 miles and turn left onto the road leading to the Long Point boat ramp. There is plenty of parking here. Because it is so secluded, be sure to lock your vehicle.

 **DIRECTIONS:**

**START:** Proceed west from the boat ramp, keeping the shore on your right side. The scenery starts out with cypress and some pine trees. As you progress, it gets more and more marshy. You will most likely see many wading birds during the warmer months, and ducks and geese during the colder ones. Birders will enjoy the many warblers and other songbirds found here.

**MILE 3.0:** At **Long Point** turn right (northeast), keeping the shore on your right.

**MILE 5.0: Haulover Point** is a shallow sand spit that leads to **Albemarle Sound.** If the water is high enough, you may be able to paddle through, but you will most likely need to get out of your boat to pull it over this sand bar.

*Durant Island*

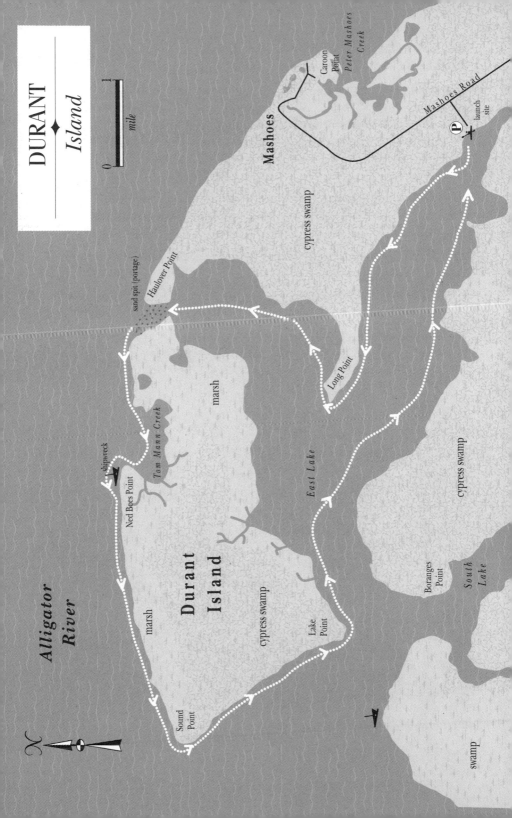

**MILE 6.0:** Watch out for pilings under the water at a small cove called **Tom Mann Creek.** They can cause you to upset your boat.

**MILE 6.75:** The **shipwreck** is just west of the other side of the cove. Continue west, keeping the shore on your left. If the wind is from the north or northeast, this may be a difficult paddle. This area is mostly marsh with some higher areas as you near the far west side of the island. This is the area where the wolves were kept restrained in pens until their release.

**MILE 9.75:** Continue around **Sound Point** at the west side of the island. Keeping the shore on your left, paddle another 2 miles until you reach **Lake Point.**

**MILE 11.75:** Turn left around Lake Point and head northeast into **East Lake.**

**MILE 13.0:** Once you reach East Lake, turn right and paddle east, following the southern shoreline for 4.5 miles to the launch site.

# Where to Eat & Where to Stay

See Route 10, Roanoke Island. There are many restaurants to explore in downtown Manteo, on the waterfront.

# Route 13:

**━ ━ ━ ━ ━ ━ ━ ━ ━ ━ ━ ━ ━ ━ ▶**

## *Alligator River National Wildlife Refuge*

lligator River National Wildlife Refuge is a true wilderness. Red wolves prowl its forests, alligators slither under the clear black water, and black bears, bobcats, otters, and deer wander among the woods and swamp of this pristine refuge. More than 150 species of birds, including the endangered red-cockaded woodpecker, wood ducks, warblers, herons, and ospreys, make the refuge their home. It's undeveloped, remote, and left pretty much to itself.

This wilderness, only thirty minutes away from the salty, sandy Outer Banks, is the northernmost home for the American alligator. Look for them on the banks of the narrow creeks. The refuge is also home to the red wolf, once classified as extinct in the wild. Efforts by the U.S. Fish and Wildlife Service have resulted in the reestablishment of a population of fifty to one hundred wolves. The wolves are mainly nocturnal, but there have been sightings during the day.

The area started out as Dare Lumber Company's Buffalo City logging development. Buffalo City, started by three men from Buffalo, New York, was once Dare County's largest city. As many as 3,000 people lived here between 1870 and World War II. The swamp was connected to the outside world by a railroad and Milltail Creek, which was used by boats to bring in provisions and transport out logs. Its main industry during Prohibition, however, was moonshining. It was estimated that 1.5 million quarts of "East Lake Dew" made their way to the nightclubs and hotels in Baltimore, Philadelphia, New York, and Washington, D.C. When Prohibition ended, the residents turned to farming for a while but found the area unsuitable, and the city died.

Most signs of the city's early days are now all but erased. As you paddle along the trails, you can catch a glimpse of the old docks and brick foundations of this once bustling city. This 152,000-acre refuge is now owned and managed by the U.S. Fish and Wildlife Service.

**TRIP HIGHLIGHTS:** The clear black water reflecting the overhanging trees and clouds makes for some spectacular photography.

**TRIP RATING:** Beginner to intermediate. There are certain areas that are easier to paddle than others on windy days. If the wind is blowing hard southwest, Sawyer Lake can be a chore paddling back up. With a northeast wind, Milltail Creek can get quite choppy, with wind-driven waves and whitecaps. Even the most novice beginner will be able to paddle most days. The trick is to choose your route carefully. Look at a map and keep track of the wind direction at all times.

**TRIP DURATION:** Three to four hours; 6 to 10 miles, depending on the route chosen.

**NAVIGATION AIDS:** Maps of the refuge paddling trails are available. Call the refuge office at (252) 473–1131 or download a map at www.outer-banks.com/alligator-river.

**TIDAL INFORMATION:** There is no tidal range, but the wind direction can raise and lower the water significantly. Best conditions are with a light northeast or northwest wind.

**CAUTIONS:** There are alligators and black bears here. Although I've never heard of any trouble with them, it is wise to keep your distance. Water moccasins are found here and can cause some anxiety when you paddle past them in the narrow creeks of Sandy Ridge Trail. Again, give them plenty of room and you should not have a problem.

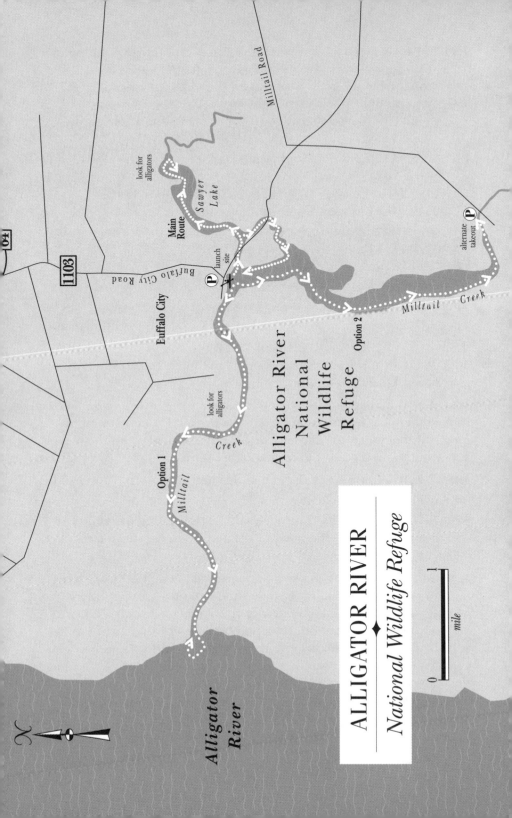

ALLIGATOR RIVER
*National Wildlife Refuge*

0 mile 1

Alligator
River

Milltail
Creek

Option 1

look for
alligators

Buffalo City

Alligator River
National
Wildlife Refuge

Option 2

Milltail Creek

alternate
takeout

**P**

launch
site

**P**

Buffalo City Road

**Main
Route**

Sawyer
Lake

look for
alligators

Milltail Road

1103

64

**TRIP PLANNING:** The ideal time to visit this refuge is during the spring or fall when the weather is cool and the insects are manageable. This is a great trip for those days too windy for the beach and the open sound. It is very well protected and possible to paddle the narrow creeks even when it is blowing a gale on the beaches.

**LAUNCH SITE:** From Nags Head take U.S. 158 to Roanoke Island where you pick up U.S. 64/264. Follow 64/264 west approximately 20 miles to Buffalo City Road (look for the sign to Buffalo City). Follow the dirt road 2 miles to the launch site.

# DIRECTIONS:

**START:** From the launch site you will see a narrow canal heading into the woods. Follow this route to where it forms a Y. You will see a trail marker here.

**MILE 0.15:** Turn left at the intersection and follow the creek as it widens into **Sawyer Lake** then narrows again.

**MILE 1.0:** You will pass through a very narrow section of slough grass here. If there has not been much boat traffic lately, the grass tends to grow together and looks like it's a dead end. The grass is just floating in a mat and you will be able to paddle right over it.

**MILE 2.0:** When you reach the end of the lake, turn around and paddle back to the Y.

**MILE 3.5:** Just before the Y, turn left and follow the trail markers. The trail meanders through the woods. Look for the large cypress trees located next to the creek.

**MILE 4.0:** You will come to a small bridge. Called **Limbo Bridge,** you will need to portage over the bridge unless the water level is very low in which case you may "limbo" underneath, leaning way, way back on the deck of your kayak. The bridge is a part of the trail system in the refuge and makes for a great hike. Keep an eye out for wolf tracks, as I've seen many here. This is near where the U.S. Fish and Wildlife Service keeps the red wolves, pending release in the refuge. If you want to try howling, you might get an answer in the distance. After you pass the bridge, follow the creek or "gut" until it rejoins Milltail Creek.

**MILE 5.0:** Stay to the right where the creek joins Milltail Creek and paddle north to return to the launch site.

**OTHER OPTIONS:**

**OPTION 1:** From the launch site, head down the short canal to Milltail Creek, which you will be able to see on your right. Once you reach the main creek, turn right and follow the creek west.

**MILE 1.0:** The banks along this section are lined with water lilies. They grow in dense mats that you cannot paddle through without getting your paddle caught up. Take the time to paddle close however, as this is where you stand the best chance of seeing an alligator.

**MILE 4.0:** Milltail Creek meets the **Alligator River.** The river is very wide and filled with submerged stumps near the shore. Turn around at this point and return to the launch site.

**OPTION 2:** For a longer trip, follow Milltail Creek south from the launch site for 5.5 miles, until it ends at the Milltail Road launch. The banks of the creek are lined with bald cypress and wild iris. I've seen white-tailed deer in the woods and black bears swimming here. To return, retrace your path to the Buffalo City launch or have a second vehicle at the Milltail Road launch for a shuttle.

# Where to Eat & Where to Stay

**RESTAURANTS**     The closest place to get food or drinks is in Manns Harbor 5 miles to the east. *White's Shopping Center* (252–473–2256) has a small grocery store, tackle shop, and a grill serving burgers, sandwiches, and snacks. **LODGING**     The closest place to find lodging is on Roanoke Island, about twenty minutes east. The following are all located on U.S. 64/264 in Manteo: *Dare Haven Motel,* (252) 473–2322; *Elizabethan Inn,* (800) 346–2466; *Island Motel,* (252) 473–2434.    **CAMPING**     RV and tent camping at *Manns Harbor Marina* (252– 473–5150) and *Cypress Cove Campground* on U.S. 64, 1.5 miles east of Manteo (252–473–5231).

*Alligator River National Wildlife Refuge*

# Alligators

Coastal North Carolina is the northernmost range for the American alligator. Once threatened by extinction due to habitat loss and poaching, the alligator has survived in the remote areas of our coastal region. American alligators are the largest reptiles in North America and can be found only in the southeastern United States. Alligators are characterized by short, rounded snouts; crocodiles have long, more tapered snouts. They can reach lengths of more than 14 feet and weigh more than 650 pounds. Alligators are afraid of people and are quite shy, but they can attack when threatened.

Alligators are rare in this area due to their metabolism. When the water temperature drops below 75 degrees, the enzymes in an alligator's gut won't properly break down food, so it eats less. During the winter, alligators move to dens or deep holes where they undergo periods of dormancy. These factors indirectly affect their reproduction and population. In North Carolina they don't reach maturity until they are sixteen to twenty years old, while in Florida they mature by the age of eight.

Although they can eat most anything, alligators concentrate mainly on fish, frogs, and small mammals as adults. They grasp their prey in their powerful muzzles, holding it underwater until it drowns, and then they swallow their food whole. There have been no known alligator attacks on people in North Carolina, but please remember to use caution around them and don't get too close.

# Route 14:

━━ ━━ ━━ ━━ ━━ ━━ ━━ ━━ ━━ ━━ ━━ ━━ ➤

## *Bodie Island*

**J**ust south of Nags Head is Bodie (pronounced *body*) Island. You won't find a bridge, because it is no longer an island. Six different inlets have come and gone in the area between Bodie Island Lighthouse and Rodanthe. The name "Bodie Island" refers to the peninsula from Whalebone Junction to Oregon Inlet. I have been told that the area got its name from all the bodies that used to wash ashore from the shipwrecks.

The current Bodie Island Lighthouse was actually the third to be built in the vicinity. The first was built south of Oregon Inlet in 1848. It lasted only ten years before another one had to be built. The second lighthouse, also located south of Oregon Inlet, was destroyed during the Civil War. The third lighthouse was finished in 1872, and is still operational today. Management of the lighthouse has just recently been transferred from the Coast Guard to the National Park Service.

The marshes surrounding the Bodie Island Lighthouse are perfect for exploring by foot or by kayak. Although you are not allowed to paddle on the freshwater ponds, there are boardwalks in place for bird-watching and an interpretive trail.

**TRIP HIGHLIGHTS:**   Great crabbing, Bodie Island Lighthouse, beautiful salt marshes.

**TRIP RATING:**   Beginner to intermediate.

**TRIP DURATION:**   Two to four hours; 7 miles.

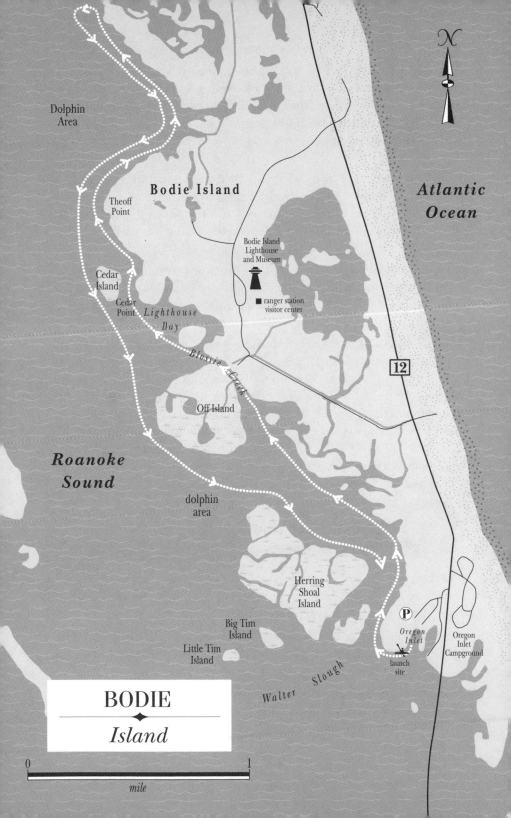

Dolphin
Area

Bodie Island

Theoff
Point

Cedar
Island

Cedar
Point

*Lighthouse
Bay*

*Blossie Creek*

Bodie Island
Lighthouse
and Museum

■ ranger station
visitor center

Atlantic
Ocean

**12**

Off Island

**Roanoke
Sound**

dolphin
area

Herring
Shoal
Island

Big Tim
Island

Little Tim
Island

*Walter   Slough*

**P**

*Oregon
Inlet*

launch
site

Oregon
Inlet
Campground

BODIE
◆
*Island*

0                                    1

*mile*

**NAVIGATION AIDS:** USCG Map NC428, Oregon Inlet, 1:24,000.

**TIDAL INFORMATION:** There is some influence from the tides due to its location just north of Oregon Inlet. Expect the water level to change with the tides to some extent. Wind direction will affect the water level more dramatically. North and east winds will create low water; southerly and westerly winds will make for higher levels.

**CAUTIONS:** This area has heavy boat traffic, including large charter fishing boats. They throw big wakes, so be aware of what's around you. Most captains are courteous and slow down before they reach you, but some would prefer to see you bounce around.

**TRIP PLANNING:** Plan your trip here with the boat traffic in mind. The large charter fishing boats return to the marina between 4:00 and 5:00 P.M. The smaller boats tend to be out all day. Getting back before 4:00 P.M. will allow you to avoid the heavy traffic and to watch the boats unload their catch at the docks.

**LAUNCH SITE:** From Whalebone Junction in South Nags Head, take NC–12 south 10 miles. Turn right just before you reach the Oregon Inlet Bridge. Keep to the right and follow the road around to the public boat ramp at Oregon Inlet Marina. You can unload your boat to the left of the ramps and then park. If you want to head out toward the bridge, keep to your left as you turn off NC–12. This will bring you to a parking area near a large propeller. This is a quieter area for launching and you will not have to cross the boat traffic.

## DIRECTIONS:

***START:*** From the launch site turn to your right (west). Keep as close to the shore as possible, staying out of the way of the motorized boats. After a few yards, you will turn right into Walter Slough.

***MILE 1.0:*** Paddle northwest toward **Blossie Creek.** This will lead you behind **Off Island,** a privately owned island with a small hunt club on it.

***MILE 1.5:*** You will see a small dock and dirt road on your right, directly across from the Off Island Gun Club. The mile-long dirt road leads to the **Bodie Island Lighthouse** visitor center.

**MILE 2.0:** Keep to the right, passing between the shore and **Cedar Island.**

**MILE 2.5:** Turn right and head north, rounding **Theoff Point.**

**MILE 3.25:** Turn around at this point, and retrace your path. Keep an eye out for dolphins in this area. They come fairly close to shore here.

**MILE 4.5:** Keep to the right of **Cedar Island** and paddle south toward Off Island.

**MILE 5.0:** When you reach Off Island, keep to the right, then follow its shoreline southeast.

**MILE 6.0:** When you reach **Herring Shoal Island,** stay to the left, passing between the island and the main shore. This will keep you out of the main boat traffic. Retrace your original route back to the launch site.

**MILE 7.0:** Take care when reaching the takeout, since this is a busy marina.

# Graveyard of the Atlantic

The North Carolina coast is famous for many things, among them history, storms, and shipwrecks. So many ships have sunk off the North Carolina coast that it is called the Graveyard of the Atlantic. There are several reasons for so many shipwrecks. The Gulf Stream, the major east coast shipping lane, goes right by the coast. Ships sometimes pass so close to the shore that you can see them from the beach with the naked eye. The problems arise when they run aground on Diamond Shoals, the sandbars off the coast that stretch out to meet the Gulf Stream.

Many ships have sunk during battle off the North Carolina coast. During both world wars, German U-boats lurked off the coast, looking for freighters and tankers to destroy. They would sit just offshore and pick off the ships as they passed between the U-boat and the shore, silhouetted against the lights of the coast.

Shipwrecks are not a thing of the past. Ships continue to run aground, caught by storms or just bad navigation. Running aground in good weather is dangerous, but during stormy weather it could be deadly. Once stuck, the waves and wind work the ship until it comes apart.

## Where to Eat & Where to Stay

**RESTAURANTS** *Oregon Inlet Fishing Center,* located at the launch site, has snacks and cold drinks (252–441–6301). *Sam & Omies* (252–441–7355), milepost 16.5, Nags Head, is a local hangout for breakfast. You have to try the crab omelette. Open for breakfast, lunch, and dinner. **LODGING** *Surf Side Motel,* NC–12, milepost 16, Nags Head, about 12 miles north of the launch site. Oceanfront, best continental breakfast on the beach. *Dolphin Motel* (252–441–7488), NC–12, milepost 16.5, Nags Head, on the ocean 12 miles north of the launch site. Rooms and efficiencies; small but nice. **CAMPING** *Oregon Inlet National Park Service Campground* (252–473–2111), directly across the street from Oregon Inlet Fishing Center.

# Route 15:

## Pea Island from Oregon Inlet

Inlets should actually be called outlets. They are formed when water, which is pushed inland by storms or wind, is suddenly pushed back toward the barrier islands when the wind changes. The force of the water is strong enough to punch a hole through the sand.

Oregon Inlet was formed during a September gale in 1846. It was named after the *Oregon,* the first ship to enter the new opening. Since it opened, the inlet has been moving steadily to the south as a result of the littoral current, which runs from north to south. This is a common occurrence, but has proved very troublesome for the small fishing vessels that use the inlet to get offshore. As the inlet gets narrower, the vessels stand the chance of running aground.

As sand accumulates south of the inlet in Pamlico Sound, it's amazing to watch the islands grow from day to day. Every time I cross the bridge, they are a little bigger, and grass is starting to grow on some of them.

Efforts to stabilize the inlet have not met with success. State and local officials are trying to gain approval from Congress to build a jetty system, but it remains to be seen if the forces of nature can be stopped here without affecting the beaches to the south.

**TRIP HIGHLIGHTS:** Exploring new islands, fishing, watching wading birds feed in the shallow marshes.

**TRIP RATING:** Intermediate to advanced, depending on the conditions and which direction the tides are running. If the tide is outgoing, I don't recommend going near the inlet.

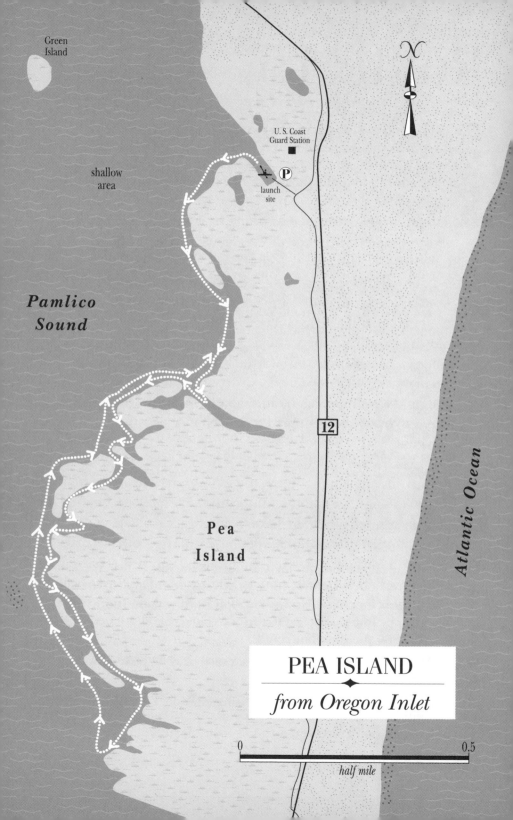

Green
Island

shallow
area

U. S. Coast
Guard Station

P

launch
site

*Pamlico
Sound*

12

**Pea**

**Island**

*Atlantic Ocean*

## PEA ISLAND

◆

*from Oregon Inlet*

0                                                     0.5

*half mile*

**TRIP DURATION:** Three to four hours; 5 miles.

**NAVIGATION AIDS:** USGS Map NC 0428, Oregon Inlet, 1:24,000.

**TIDAL INFORMATION:** There is a strong tidal influence here, due to the fact that you are so close to the inlet. At the time of an outgoing tide, use caution. The currents in the inlet can be very strong. The danger lies in the great turbulence in the main boat channel. The channel is very narrow and very deep. The depth goes from 1 foot on the shoals that line the channel to 50 feet directly under the bridge.

**CAUTIONS:** I don't recommend paddling through the inlet itself. Oregon Inlet has been closing for some time now. The only channel is deep (50 feet) and narrow and moves very fast during changing tides. It is the only route for all commercial fishing boats and can be quite dangerous for kayakers.

**TRIP PLANNING:** Watch the weather. During warm weather, thunderstorms may pop up. This area in particular is well known for forming waterspouts, tornadoes that form over the water. They can be just as deadly to boaters as a tornado. A waterspout usually dissipates once it hits land.

**LAUNCH SITE:** From Nags Head, follow NC–12 south 10 miles and cross the Oregon Inlet Bridge. Just across the bridge, on the south side, you will see a small pull off on your right. If the traffic is not heavy, you may pull over here and unload your kayak, but you will not be able to park here. The parking area is on your left.

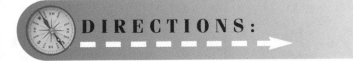

## DIRECTIONS:

**START:** From the launch site, turn left (south). If you like to fish, you can expect some great catches of flounder, spot, croaker, and gray trout. This is also a great area for collecting oysters. Some of the saltiest (they're the best kind!) can be found attached to the grass along the shore here. Continue to follow the shoreline south.

**MILE 0.75:** A tidal creek off to your left is a nice place to poke around if you have time.

**MILE 1.5:** It can be quite shallow here during low tide. Keep to the right

*Pea Island from Oregon Inlet*

of the mudflat if there is not enough water. This is a good place to view wading birds.

**MILE 2.5:** The shoreline begins to head southwest. This is where you turn around and head back to the launch site.

## Where to Eat & Where to Stay

**RESTAURANTS** *Lisa's Pizza* (252–987–2525), NC–12 in Rodanthe, about 10 miles south of the launch site, right on the sound. They brush the pizza crust with garlic butter to give it a wonderful taste. **LODGING** *Sea-Sound Motel* (252–987–2224), located 0.5 mile south of Lisa's Pizza, has efficiencies and rooms. **CAMPING** *Lisa's Pizza Campground* (252–987–2525). Camping right on the sound, with pizza and beer right next door. The ocean (one of the best surf spots around) is 0.25 mile east.

# Sedges Have Edges

The salt marsh plant communities are filled with a large variety of species. If you've ever explored a salt marsh, or any waterway for that matter, you have noticed the many different types of grasses, sedges, and rushes. As a biologist, I'm curious about the plant life around me. When I became a kayak guide I found that people I took paddling were also curious. Because my tours took place predominantly in the salt marsh, I was typically asked to explain the difference between grass, sedge, and rush. I would pass along a rhyme I learned while in college: Sedges have edges, rushes are round, and grass has a hole in the middle. This helps me remember that grasses have jointed, hollow stems, sedges have solid triangular stems, and rushes have solid round stems.

# Route 16:

━ ━ ━ ━ ━ ━ ━ ━ ━ ━ ━ ━ ━ ➤

## Pea Island National Wildlife Refuge from New Inlet

**P**ea Island is another of those places on the Outer Banks that is no longer an island. Pea Island was once cut off by one of several inlets, which have opened and closed over the years. One of those, New Inlet, was opened during a storm in 1933, with two separate passages. The residents of Hatteras Island built narrow wooden bridges across both passages to permit them to drive up the beach. The inlet closed soon after the bridges were built and they were not used again. Their remains still stand.

**TRIP HIGHLIGHTS:** Spectacular at sunrise or sunset; abundant waterfowl and beautiful scenery—take your camera.

**TRIP RATING:** Beginner to intermediate.

**TRIP DURATION:** Three to four hours; 4 miles.

**NAVIGATION AIDS:** USGS Map NC0564, Pea Island, 1:24,000.

**TIDAL INFORMATION:** There is a slight tidal influence here due to its close proximity to Oregon Inlet. The biggest tidal factor, however, will be from the wind. Check the tide tables and wind direction. The water will be very low during an east wind and very deep during a west.

**CAUTIONS:** This trip can be very difficult during windy weather because it is more open than some trips. There is not much protection during a thunderstorm, so keep an eye on the weather.

**TRIP PLANNING:** If you want a different experience, try this route at night during the full moon. It's breathtaking. This is also a wonderful trip during the fall waterfowl migration. Ducks, geese, and swans flock here by the thousands and stay all winter.

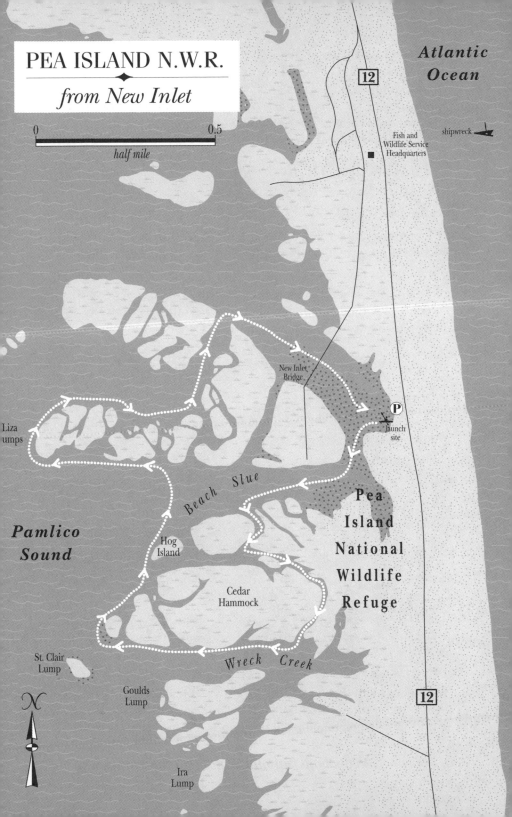

**LAUNCH SITE:** Cross Oregon Inlet Bridge to Pea Island, and follow NC–12 south for 7 miles. The pull off comes after a bend in the road, where a small sign says NEW INLET. Take a right here. You can unload your kayak right next to the ramp, but don't block it. There are no rest rooms at the put in, so you might want to stop at the visitor center 2 miles north of the launch site.

# DIRECTIONS:

**START:** From the launch site, turn left (south). Paddle a few yards and you will see the channel on your right. Turn here into **Beach Slue.**

**MILE 0.5:** Take a left at the second creek. Don't worry about making a mistake, since the first creek dead-ends shortly. This area is great for bird-watching. Travel between the shoreline and the island on your right, then turn left (east) to paddle around **Cedar Hammock.**

*Pea Island National Wildlife Refuge from New Inlet*

***MILE 1.0:*** Take a right into **Wreck Creek.**

***MILE 1.5:*** Wreck Creek opens up into the Pamlico Sound. Paddle straight out into the sound, past the small last small island on your right and turn right (north).

***MILE 2.0:*** Paddle past **Hog Island** on your right and cross Beach Slue. When you reach the shore, turn left and paddle west until you reach **Liza Lumps.**

***MILE 2.75:*** Paddle around Liza Lumps and head east, keeping the shore on your right.

***MILE 3.25:*** When you paddle as far as you can straight east, turn toward your left (northeast), through the largest channel. You will be able to see open water through the opening.

***MILE 3.5:*** When you reach the end of the channel, turn right (southeast). You should be able to see the remnants of **New Inlet Bridge.**

***MILE 3.75:*** Pass under the bridge and continue paddling southeast 0.25 mile to the launch site.

***MILE 4.0:*** When you reach the ramp, pull your boat onto the grassy area. Many kayak tour operators from all over use this ramp during the summer months and there are commercial fisherman who use it to pull up their small boats, so it can get very crowded.

***OTHER OPTIONS:*** There are several side trips you can take if you have time, or wish to return. From the launch site, turn right instead of left. You can paddle north along the shore until you reach the freshwater impoundments on your right at mile 2. This is a pleasant trip, with several nice sand/shell beaches where you can exit your kayak to stretch your legs. To return to the launch site, turn around and keep the shore on your left side.

## Where to Eat & Where to Stay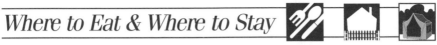

See Route 15, Pea Island from Oregon Inlet.

# Marsh Mallow

I bet you're thinking, "What the heck is a sidebar on marshmallows doing in a kayak guidebook?" Well, what we now call a marshmallow actually originated in the salt marsh. The rose mallow or marsh mallow is a perennial that grows in fresh and brackish marshes. Reaching heights of 3½ to 7 feet, it has hairy stems and is covered with large, showy, pink or white five-petaled flowers. (In our area we have the swamp rose mallow with pink flowers.) The flowers have a purple or red center and bloom most of the summer in North Carolina.

The roots of the marsh mallow are white and spongy. Years ago, people would grind the roots and mix in some sugar to create the precursor of the modern-day marshmallow.

# Route 17:

▬▬ ▬▬ ▬▬ ▬▬ ▬▬ ▬▬ ▬▬ ▬▬ ▬▬ ▬▬ ▬▬ ⟶

## *Atlantic Ocean Surf Spots*

**T**here is nothing like riding the waves. You can be in a kayak, on a surfboard, on a body board, or on your stomach. The thrill is more than just riding them in. It's punching out through the surf zone and paddling out, maybe even catching some air as you ride up and over an incoming wave. It's waiting for that one perfect ride, bobbing out beyond the beach while dolphins swim around you. It's the adrenaline rush of racing down the face of the wave, then turning around and doing it all over again.

Practicing proper surf etiquette is extremely important. Paddle surfers must share the waves with board surfers, swimmers, and other boaters. In some areas, surfers are very territorial and do not like others invading their turf.

**TRIP HIGHLIGHTS:** Adrenaline pumping double overhead waves, or mellow ankle slappers, it's all good.

**TRIP RATING:** Intermediate with sit-on-top kayak, advanced with decked white-water kayak.

**TRIP DURATION:** Each trip will vary, depending on wave and weather conditions. I've been out as long as three hours at a time when there is a swell, and I know folks who stay out all day, with very few breaks. To each his own.

**NAVIGATION AIDS:** ADC Map of the Outer Banks.

**TIDAL INFORMATION:** Look at a tide table before heading out. Make sure you get the tide for the proper area on the beach. The best surf is two hours before to two hours after a low tide.

**CAUTIONS:** This chapter is not to be taken as a replacement for surf kayak instruction. It merely lists some good surf spots. Make sure you wear the proper safety gear, including a PFD and a helmet.

Surf kayaking should only be attempted by experienced paddlers. Inexperienced paddlers can easily lose control of their boats. They can take out anyone in their path as they are pushed to shore in the soup.

Here are the rules of surf etiquette:

- Don't paddle out directly in front of anyone riding the waves. Paddle out to the side, and move if someone comes toward you.

- The wave belongs to the first surfer to catch it.

- If two or more surfers catch a wave at the same time, the one closest to the peak or steepest part of the wave has the right-of-way.

- Once a surfer is on a wave, don't try to catch the same wave. Wait for the next one.

- When you are riding on the wave, you must take evasive action to avoid other surfers and swimmers.

**TRIP PLANNING:** If you are unsure of your roll or paddling skills in the surf zone, you might want to try a sit-on-top kayak first. These are perfect kayaks to learn in or use to boost your

confidence. Almost anyone who can use a paddle can get out in
the surf and start paddling right away in a sit-on-top kayak. Be sure
to use a paddle leash.

Before you head out into the surf, you will want to watch the waves
for a while. Notice how they are breaking, how the sets are timed,
and how far offshore they break. Notice which direction the wind is
blowing. An offshore wind will tend to "stand up" the waves, while
an onshore wind will make them break sooner. The best thing to
do is visit a paddle shop or surf shop and ask a local surfer where
the best breaks are when you are there.

LAUNCH SITE: Listed here are several good surf spots in the Outer
Banks area. These locations have a good offshore sandbar, a pier,
or a landform that creates a natural break, such as Cape Point.
Keep in mind that sandbars move. A storm could cause a break to
disappear overnight.

*Atlantic Ocean Surf Spots*

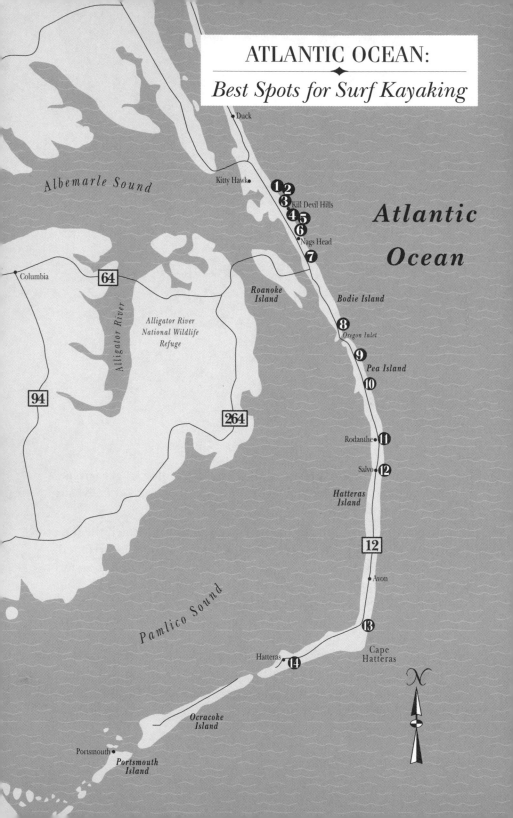

# DIRECTIONS:

All of these surf spots are accessible from NC–12 or the Virginia Dare Highway:

1. **Avalon Pier,** Kill Devil Hills.

2. **Third Street,** Kill Devil Hills.

3. **First Street,** Kill Devil Hills.

4. **Ramada Inn,** directly off the hotel, Kill Devil Hills.

5. **Bonnett Street Public Access Area,** Nags Head.

6. **Nags Head Pier,** north side, Nags Head.

7. **Jennettes Pier,** north side, Nags Head.

8. **Oregon Inlet.** You will need a four-wheel-drive vehicle for this spot. From the beach access road, turn north toward Coquina Beach. There is a good break about halfway to Coquina. If you turn south, there are several good breaks just north of the inlet.

9. **Pea Island,** on Hatteras Island. Cross the Oregon Inlet Bridge and turn into the first parking lot on your left. There is a good break just north of this access. On Pea Island, keep an eye out for cars on the side of the road. This usually means surfers have found a good break here.

10. **Pea Island S Curves,** on Hatteras Island. The S curves are just north of Rodanthe. This is a good break, but usually loaded with surfers.

11. **Rodanthe Pier,** just north of the pier, Rodanthe, Hatteras Island.

12. **Salvo,** Hatteras Island. Take the first beach access once you leave Salvo. The best breaks are south of the road.

13. **Cape Point,** Buxton, Hatteras Island. A classic spot, but there are so many other surfers you'll wait a long time for a wave.

14. **Frisco Pier,** Frisco, Hatteras Island. Surf south of the pier. This break is great with south winds. The water is much warmer than farther north.

# *Where to Eat & Where to Stay*

See other chapters for places to eat and stay in the area you choose to surf.

# Jellyfish

Jellyfish come in all shapes and sizes. The most common jellyfish on the North Carolina coast is the stinging or sea nettle, and this species causes the most aggravation. Appearing here first in June and early July, significant numbers often appear after strong southeast winds. The nettles usually disappear during September. The stinging nettle is usually white, but some have red- or purple-streaked umbrellas or red tentacles. Color makes no difference: They all sting.

The Portuguese man-of-war is another dangerous but infrequent visitor. Blown onto beaches by storms and offshore winds, the man-of-war's toxin is extremely venomous. This animal is easily identified by its purple, blue, and pink balloonlike float and long tentacles. Stay away from this one.

Exercise care when handling beached jellyfish. Although the animal is dead, the stinging cells or nematocysts can still deliver a painful sting.

If you are stung by a jellyfish, apply a solution of diluted ammonia or vinegar to relieve the sting. You may also make a paste from meat tenderizer (the plain type) and spread it onto the affected area. The properties of the tenderizer break down the walls of the stinging cells and bring relief.

For severe stings, call for medical assistance. Wash the area with cool salt water. Try to remove any clinging tentacles, with gloves if possible. Pour alcohol, diluted ammonia, or vinegar over the injured area. Dust the area with a dry powder (flour, baking soda, etc.), which the stinging cells will adhere to. Carefully scrape off the powder with a knife or edge of a shell and wash the area again with salt water.

# Route 18:

▬ ▬ ▬ ▬ ▬ ▬ ▬ ▬ ▬ ▬ ▬ ▬ ▬ ▬ ➡

## Clarks Bay from Salvo

**R**odanthe, Waves, and Salvo are three small towns on NC–12 that seem to blend together. It's very hard to tell where one stops and the other begins.

The name Salvo originates from an incident during the Civil War. Once called Clarksville, a naval officer told his crew to "give it a salvo," meaning a wave of gunfire. The name has stuck to this day. Things don't change much here from year to year, at least as far as traditions go. The folks around here still observe "Old Christmas" on the night of January 5, a carryover from Epiphany, which is celebrated January 6.

As you near the end of civilization and reenter the National Park Service property, you will see a beach access on your left. The field on your right used to be a National Park Service Campground, but it was closed due to lack of funding.

**TRIP HIGHLIGHTS:** Secluded; you will most likely have the area to yourself.

**TRIP RATING:** Beginner.

**TRIP DURATION:** Three to four hours; 3 miles.

**NAVIGATION AIDS:** USGS Map NC0634, Rodanthe, 1:24,000.

**TIDAL INFORMATION:** No tidal influence except for wind tides.

**CAUTIONS:** Wicked little prickly pear cacti seem to hide in the grass at the launch area. Wear shoes.

**TRIP PLANNING:** The launch area has picnic tables and a grill if you want to make a day out of kayaking and eating. There is a great little white sand beach for relaxing. Make sure you bring plenty of water, food, and adequate sunscreen, as well as a hat and sunglasses. During the summer months insect repellent is highly recommended.

**LAUNCH SITE:** The launch is located just south of the town of Salvo, off of NC–12. Once you leave Salvo, you will see a beach access ramp on your left. Just after this, take a right turn into a large field and follow the road around to the right. There is a parking area for the sound access. You will need to carry your boat a short distance to the beach launch site.

**START:** Just north of the launch site, there is a very nice but very short creek. This is a great place to see some egrets and herons. While you are in this area, keep an eye out for the diamondback terrapin. Fairly rare now, they used to be found by the hundreds. They were used for turtle soup and were hunted to near extinction. Once you have explored this area, return to the mouth of the creek and turn left (south), following the shoreline.

**MILE 0.5:** Turn right at the southern end of **Clarks Bay** and paddle northwest for 0.25 mile. Turn left to follow the shoreline south.

**MILE 1.0:** As you paddle along, stay as close to shore as possible, since this is where you will see most of the wildlife.

**MILE 2.0:** You are approaching No Ache Bay on your left and **No Ache Island** on your right. Turn left into **No Ache Bay.** This bay has many small creeks that harbor a wide variety of birds and other wildlife.

**MILE 2.5:** Paddle around the southernmost point of No Ache Island. Return to the shore, then retrace your route to the launch site.

**OPTIONAL ROUTE:** From the launch site, head to your right (north) and paddle toward the towns of Salvo, Waves, and Rodanthe. There are many canals and creeks to explore. Paddle for as far north as you wish, before returning to the takeout. You can't get lost, since all you have to do is keep the shore on your left side as you return.

*Clarks Bay from Salvo*

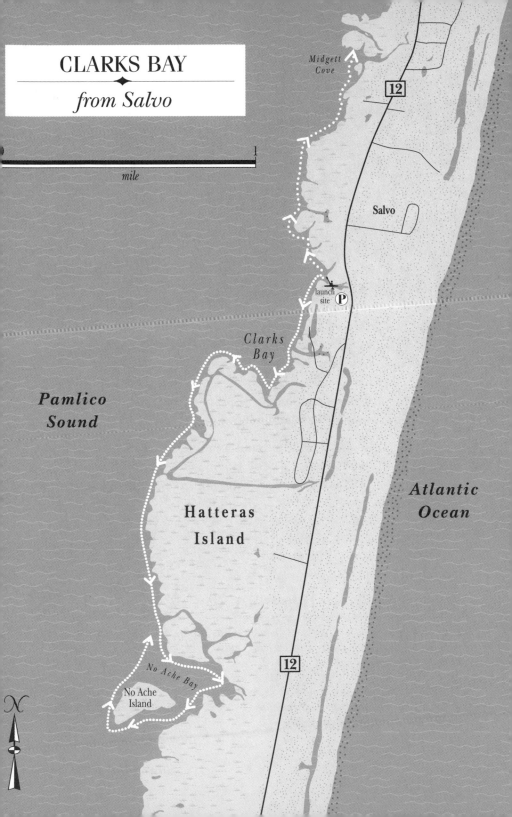

# CLARKS BAY
## from Salvo

mile

Midgett
Cove

**12**

Salvo

launch
site **P**

*Clarks
Bay*

**Pamlico
Sound**

**Hatteras
Island**

*Atlantic
Ocean*

*No Ache Bay*

No Ache
Island

**12**

N

# Chicamacomico

Located in Rodanthe, Chicamacomico was one of the Outer Banks' original seven lifesaving stations. It was opened in 1874 and was credited with saving many sailors, including the crew of the *Mirlo*. Today the Chicamacomico Historical Association, a nonprofit organization, operates the station. Volunteers staff the museum, which is full of lifesaving artifacts and awards.

Every Thursday during the summer, living-history reenactments of a beach apparatus drill are held. If you get a chance to see this, you won't regret it. The volunteers are informative and the demonstration is entertaining.

## Where to Eat & Where to Stay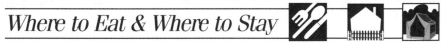

**RESTAURANTS**   *Moon over Hatteras Cafe,* NC–12 in Rodanthe, (252) 987–1080. *Bluewater Grill & Wine Bar,* NC–12 in Rodanthe, (252) 987–1300. **LODGING**   On NC–12 in Rodanthe, you'll find *Hatteras Island Resort* (252–987–2345 or 800–331–6541) on the ocean and *Sea-Sound Motel* (252–987–2224) on the sound.   **CAMPING**   *North Beach Campground* (252–987–2378) and *Cape Hatteras KOA* (252–987–2307 or 800–562–5268) are both on the ocean on NC–12 in Rodanthe.

*Clarks Bay from Salvo*

# Route 19:

---------------------------➤

## Avon from Spence Creek

Avon was once named Kinnakeet, but the post office deemed the name too long and changed it. The area was once covered with thick woods of live oak and cedar. These trees were cut as timber for building beautiful clipper ships in the early 1800s. Once cut, the trees never regrew. "Blowout" areas formed small sand dunes that began to move across the banks. These dunes covered everything in their path, including the forests. Today, woods are found only in Avon Village and a few other spots. Hunt clubs were built between Avon and Buxton and used quite heavily. Storms and disuse hastened the destruction of these buildings, but the ditches and dikes for the old ponds are still around.

**TRIP HIGHLIGHTS:** Clear water, beautiful salt marshes, secluded beaches.

**TRIP RATING:** Beginner to intermediate.

**TRIP DURATION:** Three to four hours; 5.75 miles.

**NAVIGATION AIDS:** USGS Map NC0414, Little Kinnekeet, 1:24,000.

**TIDAL INFORMATION:** No tidal influence.

**CAUTIONS:** If you paddle near Canadian Hole, you may have to dodge windsurfers. This area just south of Avon is considered a mecca for Canadian snowbirds. As many as fifty windsurfers at a time may be on the water in this spot.

**TRIP PLANNING:** This area is very secluded during the off-season. You may see many homes while paddling, but the majority of them are vacation homes, inhabited only during the summer. Always be

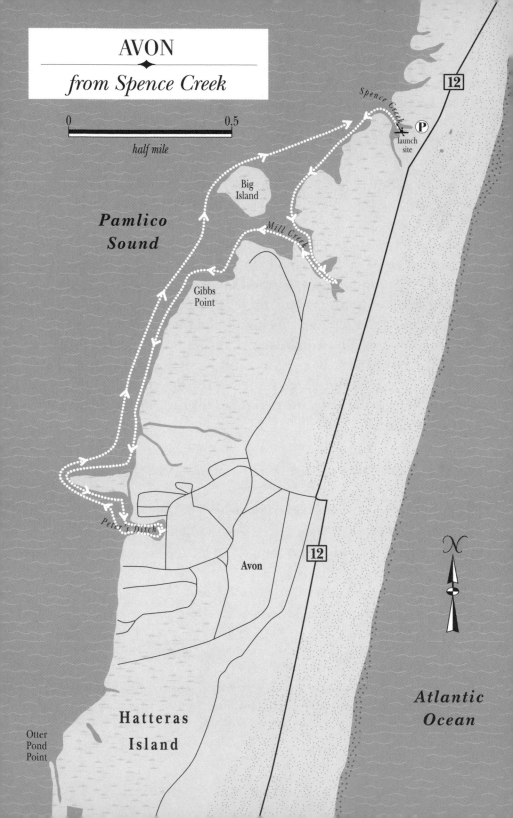

prepared. The area offers little protection from the elements. Wind is almost constant during the fall, winter, and spring; in summer, the heat can be fierce. Bring plenty of water, sunscreen, a hat and sunglasses, and food. The weather can change in a few minutes. Always carry the proper safety gear in your kayak and check the weather.

**LAUNCH SITE:** From Avon take NC–12 north. Pass the building that houses Surf or Sound Realty and take the next dirt road on your left. Follow the road a short distance until it ends on the sound. The road is a little bumpy, and if it has rained you may encounter some large puddles, so be careful. To reach the second launch site, take NC–12 to the stoplight in Avon and turn right. You will come to a small harbor, where there is a public boat ramp to the left.

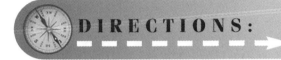

# DIRECTIONS:

**START:** From the launch site, paddle out **Spence Creek** to **Pamlico Sound** and turn left (south).

**MILE 0.5:** Keep to the left (east) of **Big Island.** Paddle southeast into **Mill Creek.** This area is great for spotting egrets, herons, and other wildlife, and for crabbing or fishing. The creek will take you into the town of Avon. During the summer months, keep an eye out for Wave Runners and other motorized boat traffic here.

**MILE 0.9:** You can purchase fish, crabs, and clams in Avon. I recommend checking out the availability and then returning with your vehicle. Turn around and paddle back up Mill Creek, heading northwest.

**MILE 1.0:** As you exit Mill Creek, turn left and paddle southwest toward **Gibbs Point.**

**MILE 1.25:** Round Gibbs Point and follow the shoreline south.

**MILE 2.0:** Paddle around the point of land that juts out into the sound. Just on the other side of this are **Peter's Ditch** and the small **harbor of Avon.** The harbor is home to a fish company, a watersports company, and various commercial fishing vessels.

**MILE 2.75:** Once you have explored this area, return to the mouth of Peters Ditch, paddle north around the spit, and retrace your route along the shore to Gibbs Point.

*Avon from Spence Creek*

**MILE 4.0:** From Gibbs Point, paddle north toward Big Island and pass to the left of it. Once you pass the island head back to your right (east) and paddle 0.5 mile back to Spence Creek and the takeout.

## Where to Eat & Where to Stay

**R E S T A U R A N T S** *Dirty Dick's Crab House,* NC–12 (252–995–3708) is located next to the Avon pier. If you want steamed, spiced crabs, this is the place for you. **L O D G I N G** *Avon Motel* (252–995–5774) NC–12, has rooms and efficiencies. **C A M P I N G** *Kinnakeet Campground,* off NC–12 in Avon, next to Avon Shopping Center. Open year-round.

*Avon from Spence Creek*

# Gull Shoals

In the sound just north of the town of Avon and south of Rodanthe lies a small island. The name Gull Shoals was originally given in 1794 to an area on Hatteras Island, approximately 5 miles south of Rodanthe. Later, the small island was also called Gull Shoals. Years later a lifesaving station was built on the beach in this same area. Originally named Cedar Hummock, it too was later changed to Gull Shoals. Today there is a small fishing and hunting shack located on the island. You can paddle out and explore it if you wish. Three miles south of the Salvo day-use area (off of NC–12) you will see a dirt road on your right, leading to the sound. It is quite rutted but passable if it is dry. Park here and spend a day exploring.

# Route 20:

------→

## *Cape Hatteras National Seashore*

**W**here sea, sand, nature, and people come together in an uneasy mix—that's a good way to describe Cape Hatteras. It's not easy to get here, to live here, or to leave. It's wild and untamed. The land is never really owned, just borrowed until the next nor'easter or hurricane.

Cape Hatteras is now a vacationer's paradise, but it was once a captain's nightmare. Two currents come together here: the Labrador Current, which flows north to south, and the mighty Gulf Stream, which runs south to north. They collide just a few miles off Cape Point at the Diamond Shoals. Sometimes this is a gentle mix; sometimes they come together with such force that they throw fish and shells far into the air, sink ships, and flood the land.

This is the heart of the area known as the "Graveyard of the Atlantic." More than 1,000 ships have sunk off the shores of the Northern Outer Banks, the victims of shallow shoals (sandbars close to shore), storms, and war. Ships tried to take advantage of the north- or south-flowing currents that passed nearby to speed their journey. Some never completed their trip and were blown aground by fierce nor'easters and hurricanes. Even today, ships are lost every year off the North Carolina Coast.

If you get a chance, walk the beach a while. The shelling is great, and sometimes the waves uncover what they once claimed. I've walked on the beach during the winter and spring and come upon shipwrecks uncovered where there was once just sand, only to return the next week to find it covered back up again.

The salt marsh on the sound side of Buxton is protected from the wind. The water is very clear and full of fish and shellfish. This is where the "Lost Colony" supposedly ended up. Artifacts such as arrowheads and other remains of an Indian village can be found in the clear, shallow water. I've found several arrowheads in the peat very close to the shore. The Indian village is now underwater, so you will need to look there. An east wind will blow the water out of the sound and make for easier hunting.

**TRIP HIGHLIGHTS:** This area is noted for its clear water, Indian history, and windsurfing. The launch site is known as "Canadian Hole." It got its name from all the folks from Canada who come to the Outer Banks to windsurf. They fill the parking lot to overflowing during the windy spring and fall months.

*Cape Hatteras National Seashore*

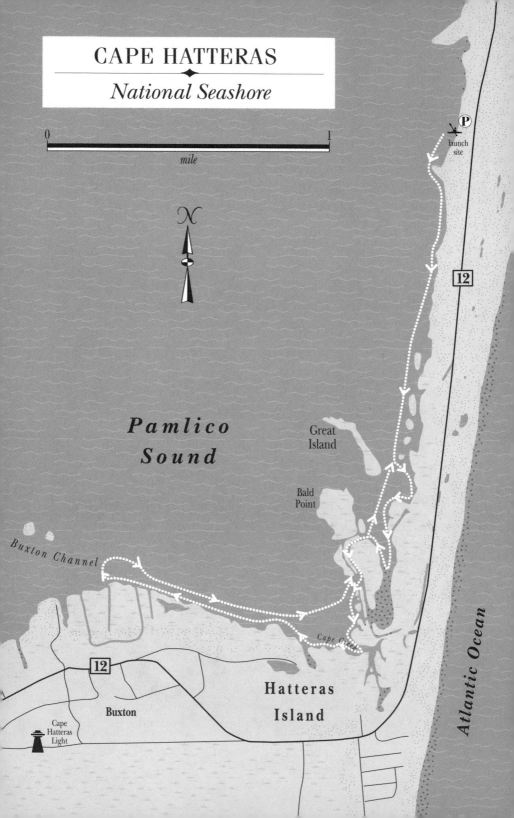

**TRIP RATING:** Beginner.

**TRIP DURATION:** Three to four hours; 6 miles.

**NAVIGATION AIDS:** USGS Map NC0091, Buxton, 1:24,000.

**TIDAL INFORMATION:** No direct tidal influence.

**CAUTIONS:** Stingrays are common in the sound here, and stepping on their stingers can be very painful. If you need to exit your kayak in the water, make sure you have water shoes on. If you walk any distance in the water, shuffle your feet as you walk to scare off the stingrays.

**TRIP PLANNING:** It's best to plan your trip here during the summer and fall months when the weather is milder. During the more turbulent winter and spring, the winds tend to make paddling difficult. It can be quite buggy at the launch site during the summer, so bring insect repellent.

**LAUNCH SITE:** From Avon, travel south on NC–12 for 0.5 mile and look for a paved parking area on your right. If you hit Buxton, turn around; you've gone too far. You can park anywhere. There are portable toilets here, and a wide sandy beach. You can launch from anywhere on the beach.

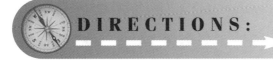

# DIRECTIONS:

**START:** From the launch site, turn to your left and paddle south, following the shoreline. Most of the wildlife will be in the marshy area along the shore.

**MILE 1.0:** As you approach Great Island, keep to your left, close to the shore. Just past the island, a small creek on the left has several branches worth exploring. Turn around when the creek dead-ends and turn left again when you reach the sound. *Note:* When I paddled this route, road crews were working on NC–12 just opposite this creek. This is the narrowest point on Hatteras Island. The creek is just a few yards from the highway, so it was a little noisy when they were working.

**MILE 1.5:** As you exit the creek, **Bald Point** is due east. Keep Bald Point on your right as you paddle. Follow the shoreline south to a longish creek on the left that is usually a good place for bird-watching. Turn around when it dead-ends. Paddle northwest toward Bald Point, turning left into the canal that curves around between islands until it opens up opposite Cape Creek (which will be on your left).

**MILE 2.5:** At **Cape Creek,** you have come as far south as possible. Turn right and head west, keeping the shore on your left. This is the area where the Algonquin Indians were thought to have lived. Keep an eye on the mudflats when they are exposed for artifacts such as arrowheads and pieces of pottery.

**MILE 3.25:** When you reach the northernmost point of the shore, turn around and paddle east until you reach Cape Creek, then turn north and retrace your route back to the launch site.

# Where to Eat & Where to Stay

**RESTAURANTS**  The *Orange Blossom Cafe and Bakery* (252–995–4109) in Buxton on NC–12 is about 2 miles south of the launch site, on the right, just past the turnoff to the Cape Hatteras Lighthouse. Get there early for the sweet rolls and bakery items. The lunch specials are to die for. Order a great big veggie or chicken burrito with rice, beans, cheese, and other great fillings, and have a picnic.  **LODGING**  *Falcon Motel* (252–995–5968 or 800–635–6911, www.outer-banks.com/falconmotel) is 1 mile south of the launch site. You can also launch from behind the motel on a small creek that leads out to the sound.  **CAMPING**  *Buxton Campground* (252–473–2111), Cape Hatteras National Seashore, 3 miles south of launch site, just past the Cape Hatteras Lighthouse.

# Route 21:

━ ━ ━ ━ ━ ━ ━ ━ ━ ━ ━ ➤

## Frisco Woods

**F**risco is a small community located between Buxton and Hatteras Village. Originally known as Trent, it is wooded on the sound side and has several large sand dunes on its ocean side. The area surrounding the Frisco Native American Museum is thought to be the site of an extensive Indian village, possibly where the lost colonists escaped to when they left Roanoke Island. The museum houses an amazing collection of Native American artifacts from around the country.

The maritime forest extends right to the sound here, creating some stunning vistas from the water, but it's the sand dunes that are the big attraction. On the ocean side, the road that leads to the Billy Mitchell Airport ends at the National Park Service Campground; it is well worth taking the time off the water to wander around the hills. The beach here is a protected bay south of Cape Point and may have calmer waters than the beaches that face northwest above Cape Point. Because of the Gulf Stream, the water here can be as much as fifteen to twenty degrees warmer during the winter months.

**TRIP HIGHLIGHTS:** Warmer water in the winter, woods that end at the water line.

**TRIP RATING:** Beginner.

**TRIP DURATION:** Three to four hours; 6 miles.

**NAVIGATION AIDS:** USGS Maps NC0091, Buxton, and NC00320, Hatteras, 1:24,000.

**TIDAL INFORMATION:** No direct tidal influence.

**CAUTIONS:** This area is known for its windy conditions, which is one of the reasons it is a mecca on the East Coast for windsurfers. During the summer months, fast moving thunderstorms can bring high winds and waterspouts. Always check the weather before venturing out.

**TRIP PLANNING:** If you plan on camping, make Frisco Woods Campground your base camp. This campground is located right on the water with wooded campsites. You can paddle right from your campsite if you wish.

**LAUNCH SITE:** From Frisco Woods Campground on NC–12 in Frisco, travel west for 3 miles. Turn right into Sandy Bay sound-side access. This access is maintained by the National Park Service and has parking, an interpretive exhibit, and a great sandy beach for launching.

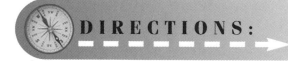

# DIRECTIONS:

**START:** From the launch site turn right and head northeast, keeping the shore on your right. This route will take you through the marshy area of Frisco sound side, which quickly turns into woods leading right up to the water.

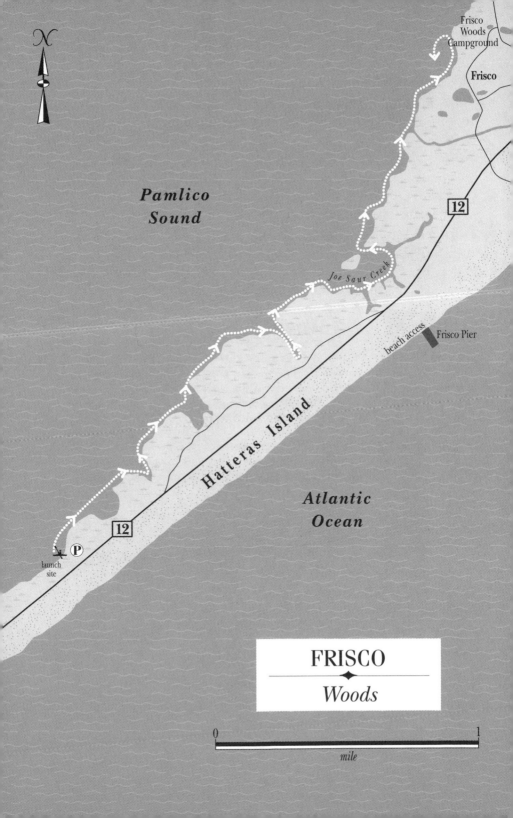

**MILE 0.5:** On your right is a nice **cove** you can explore. You may see lots of wading birds in the marsh grass and crabs in the water. This is a good area for clamming.

**MILE 1.25:** Take a right here to explore a short **canal.** Paddle until it dead-ends near NC–12. Retrace your route up the canal and turn right (east).

**MILE 1.75:** **Joe Saur Creek,** on your right, actually looks more like a small bay than a creek. You will see a small island on your left as you enter it. There are several small creeks off Joe Saur that are worth paddling before continuing north toward the campground.

**MILE 3.0:** **Frisco Woods Campground** is easy to find. There is a hard beach (grass instead of sand) lining the shore of the whole campground. There is a small rental kiosk at the eastern end of the campground. Turn around here and retrace your route back to the launch site.

## Where to Eat & Where to Stay

**R E S T A U R A N T S** *Gingerbread House Bakery* (252–995–5204), NC–12 in Frisco. This little cottage has the best pizza on the southern island. Open for breakfast and dinner Tuesday through Sunday. *Bubba's Bar-B-Q* (252–995–5421), located next to the Frisco Woods Campground on NC–12. Bubba's serves real Carolina barbecue. Order it with the coleslaw on the bun.   **L O D G I N G** *Cape Pines Motel* (252–995–5666) is on NC–12 across the street from Conners Supermarket.   **C A M P I N G** *Frisco Woods Campground* (252–995–5208), on NC–12 in Frisco, is open year-round. You can paddle up and camp on the sound in this wooded campground, which has a pool, a store, and cabins.

*Frisco Woods*

# Buxton Woods

If you visit Buxton Woods, you may not realize that you are seeing a unique area. The vegetation and freshwater ponds themselves are not unique; you are probably used to seeing the same plant and animal species back home. What makes it different is that this habitat is next to the ocean. The forest is on a ridge and swale pattern of dunes, which protects if from the effects of salt spray.

The Buxton Woods Nature Trail, which is located off the road to the Cape Point Campground, winds through woods dominated by pines, oaks, dogwoods, and blue beech. Next to them grows dwarf palmetto, a species usually associated with South Carolina. Freshwater ponds are filled with bass, bream, and turtles. The fresh water plays an important role in replenishing the underground aquifers, the only source of drinking water on Cape Hatteras.

Only part of the woods is protected within the boundaries of the Cape Hatteras National Seashore. The larger section is privately owned and being steadily developed. Time will tell if this development will eventually threaten the groundwater.

# Route 22:

**▬ ▬ ▬ ▬ ▬ ▬ ▬ ▬ ▬ ▬ ▬ ▬ ➜**

## Hatteras Island: Sandy Bay

**S**andy Bay is located between Frisco and Hatteras, near the southwest end of Hatteras Island. Life in the small village of Hatteras is slower than the rest of the Outer Banks. Residents still make their living from the sea, or from the tourists who flock to the area. The village is surrounded by salt marsh and bisected by several creeks. The largest, called "The Slash," will lead you downtown, crossing under NC–12. Farther north, Harbour Village Creek and Back Creek will take you through the residential section. It's enjoyable to spend hours exploring this quaint village.

**TRIP HIGHLIGHTS:** This is a beautiful area to paddle, with clear water, peaceful beaches, and birds and other wildlife.

**TRIP RATING:** Intermediate to advanced.

**TRIP DURATION:** Four to five hours; 8 miles.

**NAVIGATION AIDS:** USGS Map NC0320, Buxton, 1:24,000.

**TIDAL INFORMATION:** No direct tidal influence. Wind can cause water depth fluctuations.

**CAUTIONS:** The area around the Hatteras ferry docks can be very busy in the summer months. I don't recommend paddling here during the early morning or late afternoon hours when the fishing fleet is returning to port; there's too much boat traffic to paddle safely.

**TRIP PLANNING:** If you want to do something really different, try clamming. You can do it on your own with a clam rake and a cooler towed behind your kayak on an inner tube. Check at a local tackle shop for fishing and clamming regulations before heading out to the shallow water in Sandy Bay. Anchor where you can easily step out of your boat, and start raking in the soft, sandy mud.

*Hatteras Island: Sandy Bay*

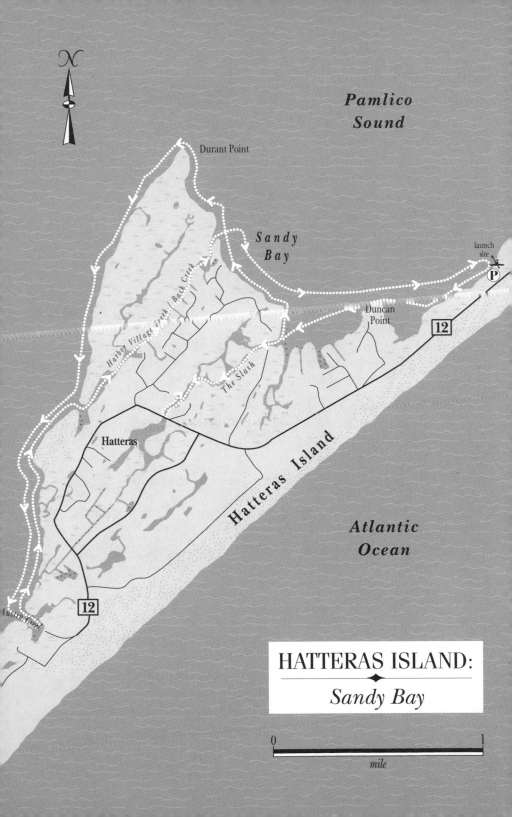

N

Pamlico
Sound

Durant Point

Sandy
Bay

launch
site

P

Harbor Village Creek / Back Creek

Duncan
Point

12

The Slash

Hatteras

Hatteras Island

Atlantic
Ocean

Austin Creek

12

## HATTERAS ISLAND:
### Sandy Bay

0                                          1

mile

There are clams everywhere here, the small cherrystone type and the larger quahog. Catch your limit and place them in the cooler until you can take them to shore, pull out your stove, and cook up some fresh, steamed clams with your favorite cold beverage.

**LAUNCH SITE:** From NC–12, park in the Sandy Bay sound-side access, which is located 0.5 mile east of Hatteras Village and 3 miles west of Frisco Woods Campground. There is a paved parking lot, an interpretive exhibit, and a sandy beach for launching.

# DIRECTIONS:

**START:** From the launch site head to your left (west). Follow the shoreline as it winds its way west and then north.

**MILE 0.5:** **Duncan Point** sticks out into **Sandy Bay.** Once you reach this point, the shoreline starts to curve west again. Follow the shore. You can rake your own clams here. The Hatteras Clamming operation provides all the equipment plus a gas burner and pots to cook them in right on the beach.

**MILE 1.0:** **The Slash** is a long creek that will take you into the town of Hatteras and up to NC–12. To explore it, turn left into the fifth canal on your left. Don't worry about getting lost; all the canals dead-end in less than a half mile.

**MILE 1.5:** At the point where The Slash meets NC–12, you can paddle up to several restaurants for lunch or dinner. Once you explore this area, turn around and paddle 0.5 mile back to where The Slash meets Sandy Bay.

**MILE 2.0:** As soon as you exit The Slash, turn left and follow the coast for 0.8 mile.

**MILE 2.8:** At **Durant Point,** turn left and follow the shore west.

**MILE 3.75:** Pass **Harbour Village Creek/Back Creek.** This creek is a mile long. Even though it is continuous, the east portion is called Back Creek and the west portion is called Harbour Village Creek.

**MILE 4.5:** Just before the ferry docks, turn left into **Austin Creek.** The creek itself still exists, but a shopping center has been built right next to it. There are several restaurants and a deli here. Once you look around as much as you wish, paddle back up the creek, turn right, and head back the way you came.

**MILE 5.5:** Take a right into **Harbour Village/Back Creek.** Paddle straight through until you exit on the Sandy Bay side.

**MILE 6.5:** Once you reach **Sandy Bay,** turn right and paddle south, retracing the route you took earlier.

**MILE 7.0: The Slash** goes off to the right; turn left to follow the shore.

**MILE 7.5:** Turn right at **Duncan Point,** and paddle 0.5 mile to the launch site.

---

# Where to Eat & Where to Stay

**RESTAURANTS** *Austin Creek* (252–986–1511), located in the Hatteras Landing shops next to the ferry docks, is definitely worth the visit. It gets my vote as the prettiest restaurant on the whole coast. The food is just as spectacular, with lots of healthy choices. *Gary's Restaurant* (252–986–2349), NC–12 in Hatteras Village, opens for breakfast at 7:00 A.M. **LODGING** *Hatteras Harbor Motel* (252–986–2565) is on NC–12 in Hatteras Village on the sound front; friendly staff. *Hatteras Marlin Motel* (252–986–2141) is also on NC–12 in Hatteras Village. **CAMPING** *Hatteras Sands Camping Resort* (252–986–2422 or 800–323–8899), on Eagle Pass Road in Hatteras Village, is open seasonally. *Village Marina Motel & Campground* (252–986–2522), on NC–12 in Hatteras Village, is open year-round.

# Cape Hatteras Lighthouse

What do you do with a 208-foot lighthouse that is in danger of being lost to erosion? You move it. In 1999, after years of controversy, the National Park Service jacked up the Cape Hatteras Lighthouse, put it on a sled, and rolled it along a track 2,900 feet inland to higher ground. The move, which was covered nationally and attracted thousands of people (many hoping to see it collapse as it was being moved, no doubt), was successful, and the lighthouse is now open for visitors to see. Much of the credit for this gutsy move goes to Robert E. Woody, Chief of Interpretation for the Cape Hatteras National Seashore. He helped make this difficult decision under heavy criticism from the press and local residents. If you are up to climbing the 268 steps to the top, you will be treated to one of the best views of the seashore. From the top, you can see the famous Diamond Shoals, and you'll get an idea of just how narrow and vulnerable these barrier islands are.

# Route 23:

━━ ━━ ━━ ━━ ━━ ━━ ━━ ━━ ━━ ━━ ━━ ━━ ➤

## Hatteras Island to Ocracoke Island

**E**arly maps show Ocracoke and Hatteras Islands joined. Hatteras Inlet was formed on a stormy night, September 7, 1846. Its history has been stormy every since. During the Civil War, the Confederates constructed two forts east of the inlet: Fort Hatteras and Fort Clark. Both these forts were attacked and surrendered to the Federal forces in 1861 and are now just bare beach. A lifesaving station that was built on the Ocracoke side of the island disappeared in 1955. The inlet has been relatively stable for the past half century. Ocracoke can only be reached by boat. A ferry provides service to Ocracoke from Hatteras Island. It still remains a trip for the hardy in anything other than the calmest conditions.

**TRIP HIGHLIGHTS:** An unspoiled island, miles and miles of beach to yourself, dolphins leading your way, wading and shore-birds by the hundreds.

**TRIP RATING:** Intermediate to advanced.

**TRIP DURATION:** Four to five hours; 6 miles one-way, return by ferry.

**NAVIGATION AIDS:** USGS Maps NC0320, Hatteras, and NC0292, Green Island, 1:24,000.

**TIDAL INFORMATION:** Check the tide charts before you go. You will need to time your crossing of Hatteras Inlet with the tides. The best time to cross is during slack tide, the time between high and low tide.

**CAUTIONS:** Heavy boat and ferry traffic and the crossing of the inlet make this a trip for intermediate to advanced paddlers. Stay close to the shore to keep clear of the ferries, which throw off huge wakes.

**TRIP PLANNING:** Time your trip so that you reach the inlet at slack tide, before the rising tide. If you miss this window, a rising tide is preferable to an outgoing tide: You will be pushed inland with a rising tide and pulled out with an outgoing one. If you do try to cross the inlet on an outgoing tide, make sure you angle north enough to compensate for the water flow. Depending on the time you cross, you may need to head north for at least a mile to counteract the outgoing flow. Under no circumstances do you want to be pulled out the inlet. This can be extremely dangerous due to the shoals.

This is planned as a one-way trip. When you reach the other side, take the ferry back to the marina or make arrangements to be met at the Ocracoke ferry docks. Although you could paddle the entire distance from the Hatteras ferry docks to Ocracoke Village, it is a 20-mile trip with nowhere in between to camp.

**LAUNCH SITE:** Take NC–12 west to the Hatteras Landing shopping center next to the Hatteras ferry docks.. Follow the boardwalk to the creek behind the shops. The dock is low to the water at the end and it is very easy to get into and out of your kayak.

# DIRECTIONS:

**START:** From the launch area paddle out **Austin Creek** to **Pamlico Sound.** Turn left and paddle west toward the ferry dock. You will need to cross the channel the ferry uses; time your trip so that you cross after the ferry has pulled away from the dock. During the warmer months there are several ferries running, so keep an eye out for all of them. Once you pass the ferry channel, keep paddling west. Keep as close to the shore as possible. It is very shallow everywhere except for the boat channel and the bottom is sandy, so you won't have any problem stopping along the way if you wish.

**MILE 1.0:** Take time to stop and beachcomb a little. The sound beaches are the best for sharks' teeth and driftwood, as well as assorted flotsam and jetsam.

**MILE 2.5:** When you reach the point where the island meets the **Hatteras Inlet,** take the time to stop and check things out. If the tide is rising, you will have a much easier crossing then if it is falling. On a

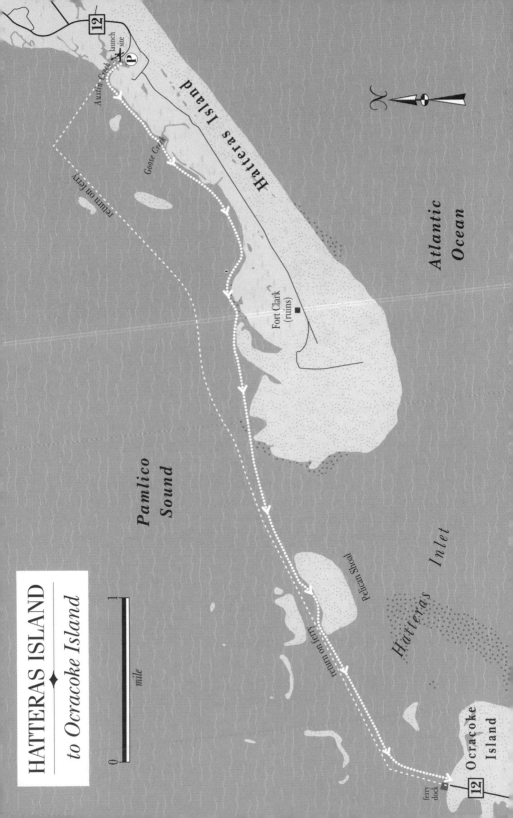

# HATTERAS ISLAND
## to Ocracoke Island

0 mile 1

Hatteras Island

Atlantic Ocean

Pamlico Sound

Hatteras Inlet

Ocracoke Island

Pelican Shoal

Fort Clark (ruins)

Austin Creek

launch site

P

Goose Creek

return on ferry

return on ferry

ferry dock

12

12

falling tide, you will need to travel quite a bit farther north. There is a sand island **(Pelican Shoal)** just north of the inlet. I suggest you head toward it and paddle around its north side before turning west and crossing the inlet. This will ensure that you don't get caught in the outgoing current and pulled out the inlet.

**MILE 5.0:** As you approach the ferry dock, you will see a large sand cliff just past the ferry terminal. Don't try to land at the ferry dock; turn left on the beach before you reach it. You can pull your kayak up on the beach. Let the ferry personnel know you plan on bringing a kayak on board when you are ready to return. The ferry ride takes forty-five minutes.

## Where to Eat & Where to Stay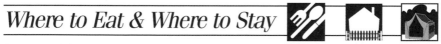

See Route 22, Hatteras Island: Sandy Bay.

*Hatteras Island to Ocracoke Island*

# Hatteras–Ocracoke Ferry

When I was a National Park Service Ranger stationed in Bodie Island Lighthouse and people would ask for directions to Ocracoke from Bodie Island, they were always confused as to why we gave distances in hours and not miles. We would tell them it was three hours to Ocracoke. They would look at their maps and see it was only 90 miles. I guess they were expecting a bridge instead of a ferry. Although Ocracoke is only a few miles from Hatteras, it can only be accessed by boat.

The Hatteras–Ocracoke Ferry makes the route every hour on the hour year-round, twice an hour during the peak summer months. A fleet of ten vessels is able to carry up to thirty cars and trucks each. After driving your vehicle onto this free ferry, you are able to get out and walk around, or stay inside if the weather is chilly. There are rest rooms on board, but no food or beverages. Many people like to stand up front and watch the hundreds of seagulls come for handouts. Passengers have been feeding them for years, and they are well trained. The trip takes only forty minutes, but you will feel like you are far away once you reach Ocracoke.

# Route 24:

---------- ➤

## *Ocracoke Island from Molasses Creek*

**O**cracoke is another world, with sand-covered lanes, quaint shops, and calm waters.Things go at a slower pace here. Area residents visit Ocracoke to get away from the hustle and bustle of the northern beaches; tourists flock here to get away from their hectic lives in other areas. Once on Ocracoke, you will find yourself slowing down to island time. You could spend the entire day doing absolutely nothing but lounging by the sea. Most people who visit here dream of returning to own a little piece of this special place.

Of course, you can opt for more active outdoor pursuits. The sound side of Ocracoke is great for clamming, fishing, and bird-watching. The marsh area is inhabited by egrets and herons. Black skimmers skim the surface of the water for food, and gulls swoop overhead. I like to go crabbing when I visit Ocracoke. All you need is a piece of string, a chicken neck, a net, and patience. Tie the chicken neck onto the string and dangle it in the water, making sure it sits on the bottom. The water is very clear here, so you should be able to see well. Once you see a crab feeding on the chicken, slowly pull up the string, having your net ready to scoop up the crab. Crabs must be at least 5 inches from one point of their shell to the other to keep. Continue until you have several dozen, then head home and feast.

**TRIP HIGHLIGHTS:** The secluded nature of the entire island.
**TRIP RATING:** Beginner.

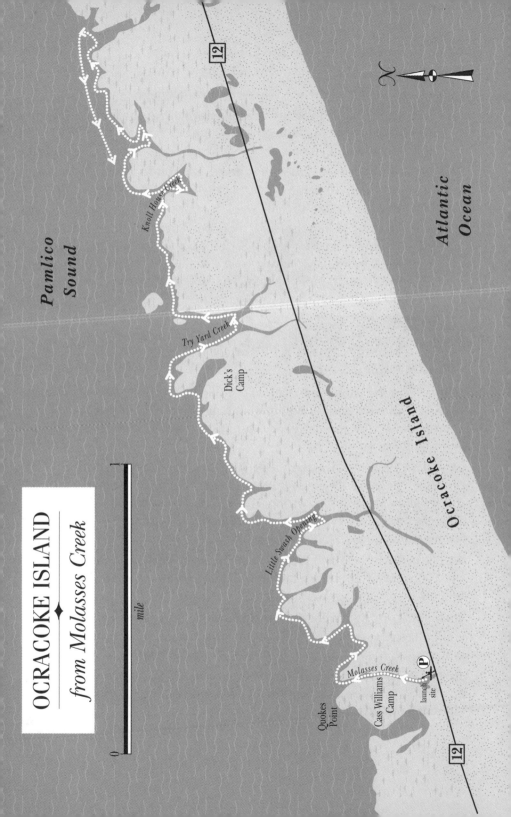

## OCRACOKE ISLAND
### *from Molasses Creek*

0 [_____] mile

*Pamlico Sound*

12

Knoll Hunter Creek

Try Yard Creek

Dick's Camp

Little Swash Opening

*Ocracoke Island*

*Atlantic Ocean*

Molasses Creek

Quokes Point

Cass Williams Camp

launch site

**P**

12

**TRIP DURATION:**   Three to four hours; 5 miles.

**NAVIGATION AIDS:**   USGS Map NC0349, Howard Reef, 1:24,000.

**TIDAL INFORMATION:**   No direct tidal influence.

**CAUTIONS:**   Bugs! If you are at all allergic to flies or mosquito bites, you should rethink paddling here. Ocracoke is a mecca for both tourists and biting insects.

**TRIP PLANNING:**   Although summer is a wonderful time here, you might want to plan your trip here during the cooler months when the insects are tolerable.

**LAUNCH SITE:**   From the ferry docks on Ocracoke Island, follow NC–12 west for 8 miles. Molasses Creek is the fourth little bridge you will come to. The parking is on the grassy shoulder, but there is plenty of room to pull off safely. The launch site is down the grassy embankment and it's very easy to reach.

# DIRECTIONS:

**START:** From the launch site, paddle out the creek a short distance until you reach **Pamlico Sound.** When you reach the sound, turn right (northeast). Follow the shoreline, keeping as close as possible for the best wildlife viewing.

**MILE 0.5:** A creek on the right leads back into the woods for a short distance. There are several of these small tidal creeks in the area, and they're great places for exploring. You will see lots of birds, marine life, and other wildlife. Once you've explored the creek, return to Pamlico Sound and continue along the coastline.

**MILE 1.0:** Turn right into **Little Swash Opening.** This creek winds back to NC–12, under the bridge and into the woodsy area. Under these bridges are great places for crabbing.

**MILE 1.5:** Turn right into **Try Yard Creek.** Once you have explored this creek, continue another 0.5 mile to the next one, **Knoll House Creek,** then paddle another 0.5 mile northeast along the shore.

**MILE 2.5:** Turn around and retrace your route to the launch site. The creeks are 0.5 mile apart; you will turn left into Molasses Creek in 2 miles. If you don't have a way of measuring distance, just count. Molasses

Creek will be the fourth large creek on your left. It is also one of the widest, so you should not have too much of a problem finding it.

## Where to Eat & Where to Stay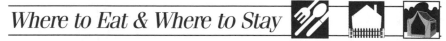

**RESTAURANTS**   The *Pony Island Restaurant* (252–928–5701), less than 0.5 mile from the town docks, is a tradition for breakfast, also open for lunch and dinner. Sit inside or outside on the patio. You cannot leave Ocracoke without a trip to *Howard's Pub* (252–928–4441), which has been open every day since 1991, serving good food and more than 200 beers to choose from. If you're looking for nightlife, this is where you'll find it.   **LODGING**   The *Anchorage Inn* (252–928–1101) offers clean accommodations right on Silver Lake. Beautiful sunsets, pool, boat ramp.   **CAMPING**   *Teeters Campground* (252–928–3135 or 800–705–5341), on British Cemetery Road, is open from March to November.

*Ocracoke Island from Molasses Creek*

# British Cemetery

The crew of the British vessel HMS *Bedfordshire* lies buried on Ocracoke Island, far from their homes. In April 1942, Prime Minister Winston Churchill sent the ship and its crew to help protect the United States from German U-boats. The ship was torpedoed on May 11, and it sank approximately 40 miles south of Ocracoke.

All hands aboard were drowned, including the four officers and thirty-three enlisted men. Four bodies were recovered when they washed ashore three days later. The grateful villagers gave the sailors a proper burial in a small plot of land.

The Coast Guard still maintains this cemetery, located on British Cemetery Road in Ocracoke Village. A British flag flies above the graves. Each year, the local military has a small celebration to honor these brave men.

# Route 25:

▬ ▬ ▬ ▬ ▬ ▬ ▬ ▬ ▬ ▬ ▬ ▬ ▬ ▬ ▬ ▬ ➤

## *Ocracoke Island: Silver Lake*

**O**riginally known as Cockle Creek, Silver Lake Harbor was established in 1931. The creek was dredged and a harbor and marina were constructed. This dredging made it possible for large vessels to come into dock, and Ocracoke Village grew into a fishing village. Ocracoke is unlike any other island on the North Carolina coast. Even though it is a bustling tourist haven, it seems to still exist in another time. The small size, the scarcity of private property, and the limited freshwater help to limit development of the island. The best way to explore Ocracoke is slowly, on island time. Don't hurry. Savor the little things and you will be able to really appreciate this jewel.

**TRIP HIGHLIGHTS:** Clamming on the north side of the island; having a slow, leisurely breakfast on a secluded beach; simply messing around in your boat with no particular place to go and no hard time schedule.

**TRIP RATING:** Intermediate to advanced.

**TRIP DURATION:** Four hours to all day—don't hurry; 8 miles.

**NAVIGATION AIDS:** USGS Maps NC00540, Ocracoke, and NC0586, Portsmouth, 1:24,000.

**TIDAL INFORMATION:** No significant tidal influence.

**CAUTIONS:** Bring plenty of sunscreen, insect repellent, and water. You will need all three.

**TRIP PLANNING:** Fall and winter are the best times to paddle here. The weather is mild, the water temperature stays in the 60s, the rates are down, and so are the bugs. Summer is gorgeous, of course, but can be rather crowded and hot, with lots of biting flies, especially on the sound side.

**LAUNCH SITE:** The launch site is on the southeast end of the island at the end of NC–12, to the right of the Ocracoke Island Visitor Center. You can drop your boat at either side of the ramp before parking your vehicle.

# DIRECTIONS:

**START:** From the launch site, turn left (south) and follow the shore. You will shortly come to the mouth of **Silver Lake.** I don't recommend paddling in the lake itself except in the off-season due to the heavy boat traffic. Cross the mouth of the lake, keeping an eye out for any boats coming or going. Once you reach the other side, **Windmill Point,** continue to paddle south, keeping the shoreline on your left. You will pass the inhabited section, where vacation homes line the shore for a half of a mile or so, before leaving civilization behind.

**MILE 0.9:** At **Springers Point,** the island starts to curve southwest. Just past the point is **Old Slough,** a marshy area that is a good place to view birds and other wildlife.

**MILE 1.25:** Continue following the shore as it bends to the right. Along the next mile, the shoreline is more woodsy, with secluded beaches. This is a great area to get out and explore, maybe pull your kayak up on the beach and hike the short distance to the oceanside beaches for great shelling.

**MILE 4.0:** Directly across the **Ocracoke Inlet,** you will see **Portsmouth Island** in the distance. Once you reach the inlet, turn around and retrace your path back to the launch site.

## *Where to Eat & Where to Stay*

See Route 24, Ocracoke Island from Molasses Creek.

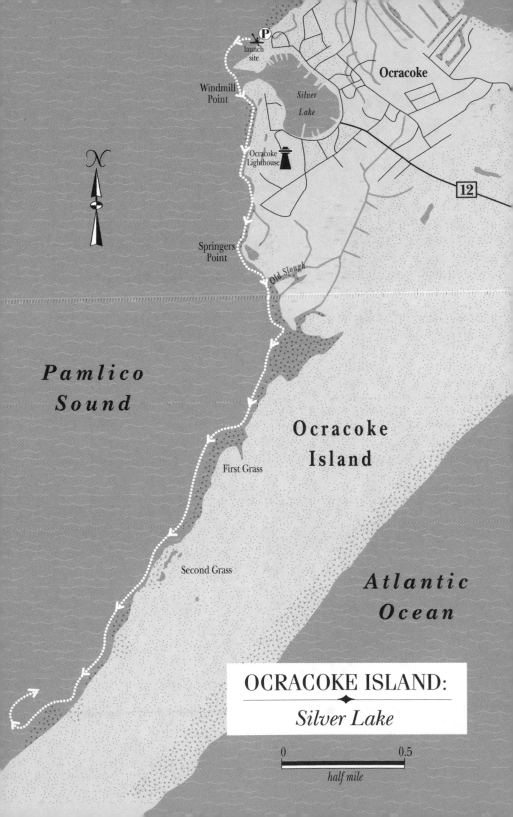

Ocracoke

launch site

Windmill
Point

*Silver
Lake*

Ocracoke
Lighthouse

12

Springers
Point

*Old Slough*

**Pamlico
Sound**

**Ocracoke
Island**

First Grass

Second Grass

**Atlantic
Ocean**

OCRACOKE ISLAND:
*Silver Lake*

0                    0.5
*half mile*

# Ocracoke Ponies

The wild ponies of Ocracoke have a questionable history. Some say they swam ashore from a Spanish shipwreck, others tell of English ships trying to lighten their load, casting them off to sink or swim ashore. Whichever tale is the truth, these sturdy little ponies have existed on the island for many years. Their number has dwindled over the years: Some were auctioned off and others died of disease. Once able to roam free, they are now penned in a large area off NC–12 about 6 miles southwest of the Hatteras–Ocracoke ferry docks. There is a small parking area and a raised platform for visitors to view the remaining two dozen ponies. You may visit them year-round, but don't try to ride them or enter the pens. Although they may look mild-mannered, they are wild and will kick and bite if you get too close.

# Core Banks

# Route 26:

- - - - - - - - - - - - - ->

## *Portsmouth Island from Ocracoke*

**T**his is one of America's few remaining undeveloped barrier islands. Covered by grasslands, bordered by dense vegetation, dunes, and wide open beaches, and surrounded by salt marsh, Cape Lookout remains virtually untouched. The earliest maps called the area "horrible headland" in reference to its dangerous shoals. The sound side, however, is a calm, sheltered anchorage. The north side of the island, near the village of Portsmouth, is mudflats and frequently overwashed. The village is no longer inhabited, except by National Park Service volunteers or those chosen by lottery to stay in one of the historic homes.

**TRIP HIGHLIGHTS:** Great shelling and snorkeling, very clear water; like being on your own deserted island.

**TRIP RATING:** Intermediate to advanced.

**TRIP DURATION:** Six hours to overnight; 8 miles.

**NAVIGATION AIDS:** USGS Map NC0586 Portsmouth, 1:24,000.

**TIDAL INFORMATION:** There is a strong tidal influence when you pass through Ocracoke Inlet. Make sure you carefully time your trip to coincide with the tides. The best time to cross the inlet is during the slack tide before an incoming tide. Tide charts are available in all the local newpapers, visitor guides, and the phone book.

**CAUTIONS:** The weather here is very changeable and the island is quite secluded. Make sure you are very well prepared both with supplies and your skills.

**TRIP PLANNING:** You can make this a day trip, but I recommend camping over. Public facilities are limited. Be sure to bring insect repellent, food and drinking water, sunscreen, appropriate clothing, and a hat. Mosquitoes may visit everywhere else, but this is where they live. The weather is unpredictable here. Fierce lightning storms are common, so be prepared. If you wish to get a ride over to the island or if the weather turns really nasty and you have to get back, you can call Captain Rudy Austin (252–928–4361 or 252–928–4281). He will take you there and pick you up for a modest fee.

**LAUNCH SITE:** From the ferry docks on Ocracoke, follow NC–12 for 15 miles through the village of Ocracoke until it ends at the public parking lot next to the National Park Service Visitor Center. You can drop your boat next to the ramp, then park in the lot. There is no charge for parking.

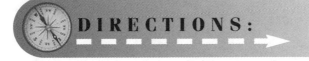

# DIRECTIONS:

***START:*** From the Silver Lake boat launch turn left and head south. Be careful of the waves from the boat traffic when you pass the opening to **Silver Lake,** especially when the large Cedar Island ferry is passing by. Follow the shore south.

***MILE 2.0:*** As you approach the inlet, the sand shoals curve north for quite a ways. Take a few minutes to scope out the conditions of the inlet before crossing. When you cross, head west, away from the inlet, for 1.5 miles. Follow the boat channel, but keep just outside of it.

*Portsmouth Island from Ocracoke*

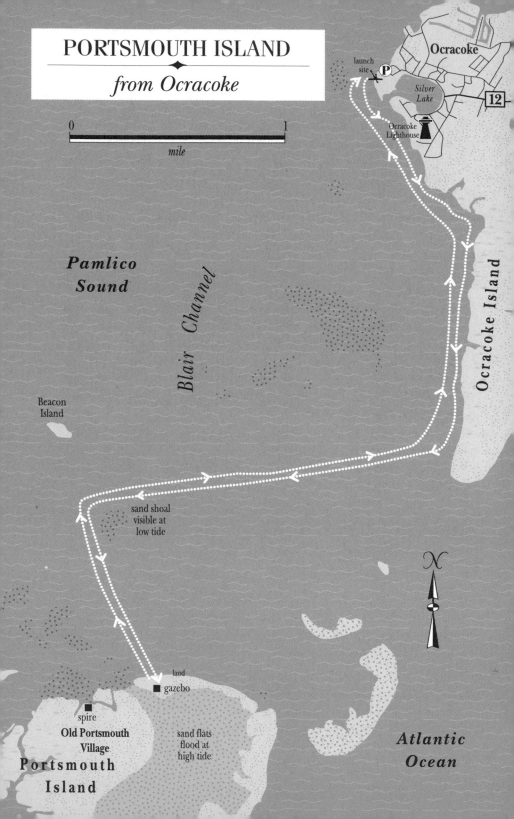

*MILE 3.5:* At low tide, there will be a sand shoal at this point. (**Beacon Island** will be due north.) Turn left and head south toward **Portsmouth Island.** From the water you should be able to spot the small gazebo to the left of historic Portsmouth village. Eventually you will want to land near here. If you have trouble spotting the gazebo, you should be able to sight the church spire in the village. I don't recommend staying in the village except during the cooler months. The mosquitos are legendary here, and can make things miserable unless you are prepared. This is a perfect opportunity to try out that mosquito netting you've thought to buy just for this trip.

*MILE 4.0:* Land on Portsmouth Island. The gazebo area is a good choice because it is open to the wind, which keeps the mosquitos under control. From here, you can paddle a short distance to visit the village or hike across the sand and mudflats to visit the beach. You are allowed to camp anywhere on the island except within 100 feet of any structure. The beach is the best spot to camp to escape the insects, but you need to be an experienced paddler to navigate the inlet to get to the ocean side. It is a long walk there from this end of the island. When you are ready to return to Ocracoke retrace your path north, to the sand bar west of the inlet, then follow the boat channel back to the Ocracoke side of the inlet. From here, simply follow the coast back to the launch site, keeping the shore on your right.

# Where to Eat & Where to Stay

There are no facilities located on Portsmouth Island. Bring everything you need. You are allowed to camp anywhere on Portsmouth Island except for the village.

# Mosquitoes

There are more than 2,000 species of mosquitoes on the planet; seventy of those live in the United States. In certain places on the North Carolina coast they can be fierce. You can thank our wild, natural areas for that. The marshy habitat of still waters and mild temperatures make this a particularly hospitable place for them. No matter where you go, there they are.

Only the female mosquito bites. Blood is necessary for her to lay her eggs. She lays up to 500 eggs at a time; luckily for us, only a few survive. If you are staying on one of the more deserted islands, you may think even a few is too many. If they are not biting, the incessant drone can make for a sleepless night if you are not prepared with a good tent and insect repellent.

Mosquitoes track their prey by sound waves and chemical traces left in the air. Dark clothing and the carbon dioxide we exhale attract the female. If you wear perfume, perspire, or just possess a smell they like, you may be a mosquito magnet.

When she zeros in on you, she lands, cuts into the skin and injects her saliva, which contains an anesthetic of sorts to deaden the area and an anticoagulant to keep your blood from clotting. You may not feel the bite until she has left and an allergic reaction kicks in.

To help avoid mosquito bites, wear long pants and a light-colored long-sleeved shirt. Try to avoid heavily scented creams or deodorants and perfumes. Use a strong repellent, which works by clogging the pores of a mosquito's receptors. The most effective repellents contain DEET, but they should be used with caution. Many people are sensitive to DEET and it can cause an allergic reaction.

# Route 27:

━ ━ ━ ━ ━ ━ ━ ━ ━ ━ ━ ━ ━ ━ ━ ➤

## Portsmouth Island from Atlantic

**E**stablished in 1753, Portsmouth grew to be the largest settlement on the Outer Banks. It remained the largest for one hundred years. At that time, Ocracoke Inlet was the major trade route through the Outer Banks. Large, heavily laden ships eventually found the inlet too shallow to sail through and were forced to transfer their cargoes to more shallow draft boats. Portsmouth was established to provide facilities for this process.

By the time the Civil War was getting started, many residents had fled to the mainland. The inlet had also begun to shoal and a new, deeper inlet was opened at Hatteras, shifting the shipping routes north. Isolation, a depressed economy, and the constant threat to homes and families from storms finalized the end of Portsmouth. The last residents on the island moved to the mainland in 1971. There remain old fishing and hunting shacks on the island that are used only during the season.

**TRIP HIGHLIGHTS:** The feeling that you are on your own private island; white sand beaches; some of the best shelling around.

**TRIP RATING:** Intermediate to advanced.

**TRIP DURATION:** Three hours to overnight; 4 miles.

**NAVIGATION AIDS:** USGS Maps NC0024, Atlantic, and NC0731, Styron Bay, 1:24,000.

**TIDAL INFORMATION:** There is a 2–3 foot tide in this area. Make sure you have a tide chart and plan your trip accordingly.

**CAUTIONS:** The secluded nature of this island demands that you plan your trip carefully and make sure you have everything you need.

**TRIP PLANNING:** Be sure to bring plenty of water, food, sunscreen, and proper safety gear.

**LAUNCH SITE:** From the Cedar Island ferry dock, follow NC–12 south for about 10 miles to Cedar Island Road. Turn left and continue 3 miles to the Morris marina and ferry dock in Atlantic. If you wish, you may take the 4-mile ferry ride over to the old ferry landing at Portsmouth Island.

**DIRECTIONS:**

**START:** From the marina, follow the ferry channel. The channel has the deepest water, which makes for a faster, easier trip. Stay next to the channel, not in it, when there is other boat traffic.

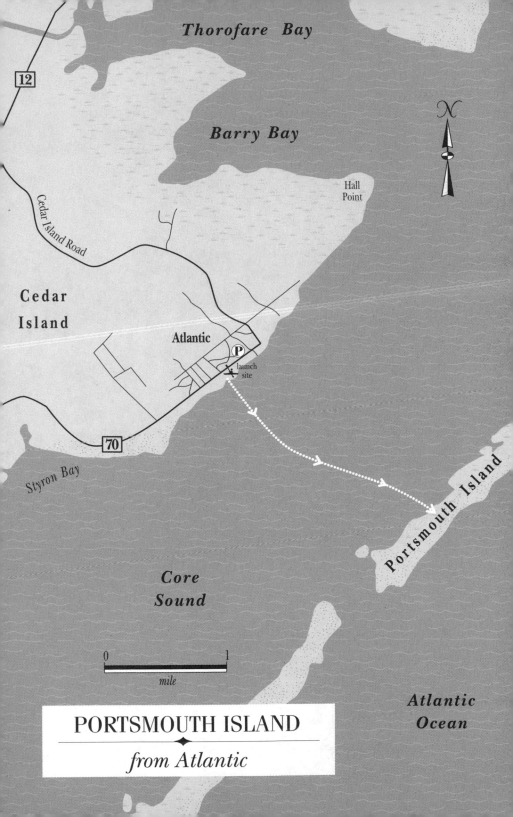

Thorofare Bay

Barry Bay

Hall
Point

Cedar Island Road

Cedar
Island

Atlantic

**P**

launch
site

70

Styron Bay

Core
Sound

Portsmouth Island

0        1
*mile*

Atlantic
Ocean

## PORTSMOUTH ISLAND

*from Atlantic*

12

# Shelling

Walk along the beaches of Portsmouth Island and you're more likely to be looking down instead of up, searching for seashells. These uninhabited beaches offer some wonderful hours spent shelling. You are likely to find whole shells here, thrown up on the beach during stormy weather. It's worth it to bring along a shell identification book or chart so you can identify what you've found. Keep an eye out for these types in your visit:

- Arks and Cockles. These shells have scalloped and ribbed shells. They are cupped or curved and are heart-shaped. You'll find many of these on the beach.

- Oyster. You'll find lots of oyster shells of all sizes. Some very large shells are remnants from the marshes that used to be where the beach is now.

- Clam. Clams of all types, from the quahog (pronounced *CO-hog*) to the smaller cherrystone, littleneck, or coquina, can be found here.

- Penshell. This fan-shaped shell is translucent, scaly, and fragile and is one of the largest you'll find.

- Whelk. Called "conch" locally, this is the shell most people want to find. There are several types to look for: lightning, channeled, and knobbed.

*MILE 2.0:* Follow the ferry channel right up to the dock on **Portsmouth Island.** If you are visiting during the warmer months, be prepared for a mosquito onslaught. They can be horrendous. As soon as you can, move your kayak over to the ocean side to set up camp. The ferry dock area is marshy with a narrow shrub zone. Although this is great as a wind block during stormy weather, you will want the wind the rest of the time to help blow the insects away. The beach is not very wide at this point, and hauling your kayak over is not too much of an ordeal.

This area used be filled with fishing and hunting shacks, built with driftwood, scrap lumber, and the like. Several years ago, the National Park Service tore them all down. It is now much more natural looking, but many fishing and hunting parties still use this area. Keep an eye out for four-wheel-drive vehicles all along the beach on Portsmouth Island.

To return to the mainland, follow the ferry channel back the way you came.

## *Where to Eat & Where to Stay*

There are no facilities for food or lodging on Portsmouth Island; plan on bringing everything you need. **C A M P I N G** There is primitive camping available everywhere on the island. There are no designated campgrounds, but no camping is allowed within 100 feet of any structure. For more information, contact the Superintendent, Cape Lookout National Seashore, (919) 728–2250.

# Route 28:

## Cedar Island
## National Wildlife Refuge

**W**hen you leave the Cedar Island ferry from Ocracoke, you will get the feeling that you are entering another world yet again. So different from the sleepiness of Ocracoke Island, Cedar Island greets you with a ferry dock and a few homes and businesses. As you drive from the ferry to the launch site, you will soon see why this is a favorite destination with sea kayakers. There are miles and miles of

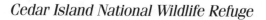

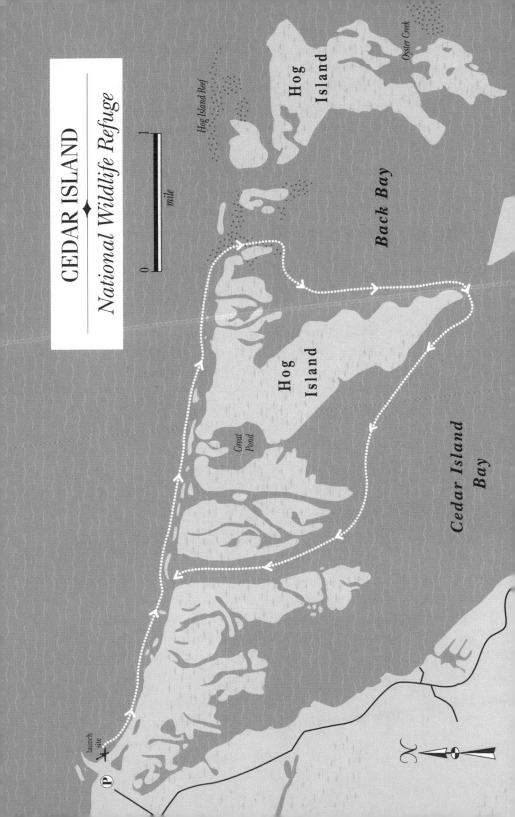

## CEDAR ISLAND
### ◆
### *National Wildlife Refuge*

mile

0 1

Hog Island

Hog Island Reef

Oyster Creek

Back Bay

Hog Island

Great Pond

Cedar Island Bay

launch site

Ⓟ

undulating cordgrass and black needlerush, looking like so many wheat fields. The road winds back and forth as you cross the marshes. These wide expanses are dotted with higher ground covered with live oaks and pines. A kayak is the perfect means to explore this watery paradise.

**TRIP HIGHLIGHTS:** Nearly 270 species of birds; miles and miles of beautiful salt marsh; undeveloped wilderness.

**TRIP RATING:** Intermediate to advanced.

**TRIP DURATION:** Four to six hours, not including the ferry ride; 7.5 miles.

**NAVIGATION AIDS:** USGS Maps NC0024, Atlantic, and NC0526, North Bay, 1:24,000.

**TIDAL INFORMATION:** No direct tidal influence.

**CAUTIONS:** Watch out for the ferry and boat traffic.

**TRIP PLANNING:** Bring everything you need for your trip, including plenty of water and food. From Ocracoke Island, you will need to take the Cedar Island ferry, which will take two and a half hours. Reservations are recommended; call (800) 293–3779.

**LAUNCH SITE:** Once you land on Cedar Island, you can park in the parking lot and launch from the public boat ramp.

# DIRECTIONS:

**START:** From the launch site, turn right and head east, following the shore.

**MILE 1.0:** Continue east, passing a channel on your right. You will be returning up this channel on your way back.

**MILE 1.75:** On your right is **Great Pond.** It's a good area for bird-watching, especially during the fall migrations.

**MILE 3.0:** Turn right at this large channel and paddle south into **Back Bay.**

**MILE 4.5:** Turn right to round the southernmost point of Hog Island. Paddle northwest toward the next point of land ahead of you.

**MILE 5.5:** Turn right into the channel and head north for 1 mile until you reach Pamlico Sound.

**MILE 6.5:** When you reach the sound, turn left and paddle the last mile back to the launch site.

## Where to Eat & Where to Stay

**RESTAURANTS AND LODGING** There is a small restaurant, motel, and campground at the ferry docks (252–225–4861). There are many motels and restaurants located in Beaufort, 35 miles south from the launch site. Try the *Beaufort Inn* on Ann Street in Beaufort with waterfront views, (252) 728–3464 or (800) 726–0321. For food: *Net House Steam Restaurant and Oyster Bar*, located on Turner Street in Beaufort, (252) 728–2002. My favorite is to hit the steamed seafood and then top it off with their awesome Key lime pie. **CAMPING** *Driftwood Campground* is located on the water at the ferry docks, (252) 225–4861.

# Cedar Island

Located at the end of NC–12, Cedar Island is accessible from Beaufort or by ferry from Ocracoke Island. The main reason people visit is for the birdlife. Waterfowl—including mallards, redheads, pintails, black ducks, and green-winged teals—are abundant all year. Other wildlife includes deer, river otters, black bears, and raccoons.

Cedar Island Wildlife Refuge was formed in 1964 to help the black duck. Impoundments were built to attract the birds. Today, the area is visited mostly during the spring, summer, and fall.

# Route 29:

----------------------------------➤

## Lake Mattamuskeet

**D**rive about ninety minutes west from Nags Head on U.S. 264 and you will be pleasantly surprised. Lake Mattamuskeet, North Carolina's largest natural lake, is a paddler's paradise. From December through February, Lake Mattamuskeet attracts thousands of swans, ducks, and geese. This 50,000-acre national wildlife refuge is the winter home of nearly half the nation's tundra swans. The first weekend in December, Lake Mattamuskeet Swan Days celebrates the return of the swans and other waterfowl.

This refuge comprises marshes, forests, and the sprawling lake that is seldom more than 5 feet deep. Duckweed and other water foliage that thrives on the quiet waters attracts the birds and blue crabs in great numbers.

This unique environment was almost ruined in 1914 when plans were made to drain and convert the lake into farmland. New Holland Farms, as it was to be called, dredged thousands of miles of canals and built the world's largest pump to divert the water. A first-class hotel was built with a full fleet of freight and passenger boats available for use. This plan did not take long to fall apart, however. Wet soil conditions, excessive rain, and the fact that the lake is several feet below sea level changed the developer's plans.

In 1934, 50,000 acres of the farm were sold to the U.S. government for developing into a wildlife refuge. The Civilian Conservation Corps helped to set up the refuge and convert the pumping plant into a rustic lodge for hunting and fishing. Mattamuskeet Lodge opened to the public in

1937 and became known as the Canada goose hunting capital of the world.

The lodge now attracts kayakers, bird-watchers, and photographers who come to see the wildlife. You will enjoy this beautiful paddle no matter what the season.

**TRIP HIGHLIGHTS:** Wading and shorebirds of all types; plenty of crabs in summer.

**TRIP RATING:** Beginner to intermediate.

**TRIP DURATION:** Full day; 15 miles.

**NAVIGATION AIDS:** USGS Maps NC0511, New Holland; NC0226, Fairfield; NC0216, Englehard West; NC0469, Middletown; NC0737, Swanquarter; and NC0514, New Lake SE, 1:24,000.

**TIDAL INFORMATION:** No tidal influence.

**CAUTIONS:** Shallow water will limit where some boats can go. The average water depth is around 2 feet. Large, fast moving thunderstorms are common during the warmer months.

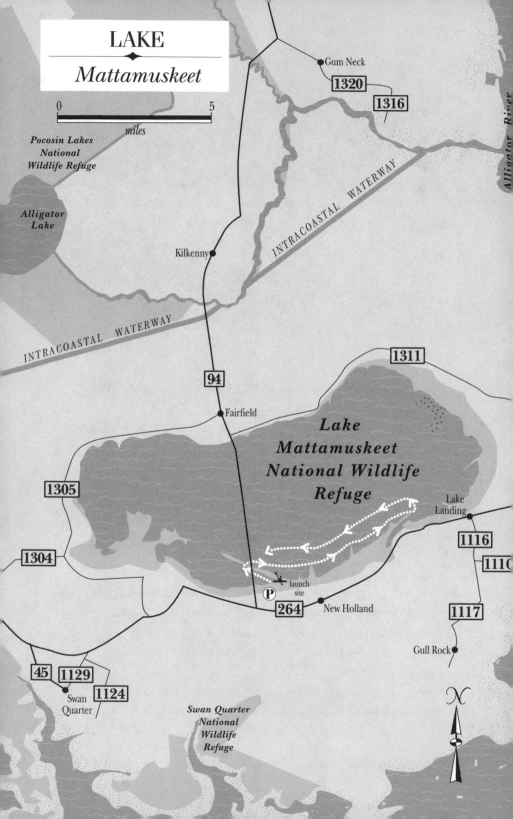

# LAKE
## Mattamuskeet

0 ———◆——— 5
*miles*

Pocosin Lakes
National
Wildlife Refuge

Alligator
Lake

Gum Neck

**1320**

**1316**

INTRACOASTAL WATERWAY

Kilkenny

INTRACOASTAL WATERWAY

Alligator River

**94**

Fairfield

**1311**

Lake
Mattamuskeet
National Wildlife
Refuge

Lake
Landing

**1305**

**1116**

**1110**

**1304**

launch
site

**P**

**264**

New Holland

**1117**

Gull Rock

**45**

**1129**

**1124**

Swan
Quarter

Swan Quarter
National
Wildlife
Refuge

N
S

**TRIP PLANNING:** Check the weather before heading out. The lake is very shallow, which affords protection from waves and wind, but storms can move in quickly. You don't want to be out in the middle of the lake during a lightning storm.

**LAUNCH SITE:** From U.S. 264 and NC–64, drive north on NC–94 for 1.5 miles to the entrance to the refuge. Turn right on the gravel road and drive another 2 miles to the boat ramp behind the refuge headquarters. There are rest room facilities at the refuge headquarters.

# DIRECTIONS:

**START:** From the ramp, paddle northwest out the canal until you reach an intersecting canal and turn right. You will paddle under the bridge and up the canal that leads to the lake.

**MILE 1.25:** Once you reach the lake itself, turn right and follow the shoreline. You will be exploring the lake's larger section.

**MILE 2.0:** The shores are lined with a combination marsh and woods. Look for songbirds in the trees along the shore.

**MILE 4.0:** The water's edge is lined with magnificent bald cypress trees, which lose their needles in the fall. These trees stain the water black with tannic acid. Known as the thousand-year wood, these trees can live for hundreds of years.

**MILE 7.5:** At this point you can take a sharp right turn. This is where you turn around and retrace your route to the bridge.

**MILE 14.0:** When you reach the bridge, paddle back under it and up the canal to the launch site.

---

## Where to Eat & Where to Stay

**RESTAURANTS** and **LODGING** The closest restaurants and lodging are located in Engelhard, 10 miles east. From Lake Mattamuskeet, follow NC–94 south to U.S. 264. Turn east and follow 264 to NC–1109. **CAMPING** *Riverside Campground* (252–943–2849) is located 25 miles east on U.S. 264 between Lake Mattamuskeet and Belhaven.

# Shackleford Banks

# Route 30:

------------------------------------------→

## Cape Lookout National Seashore

So close to civilization, yet so far away, Cape Lookout National Seashore is another world. This 55-mile-long seashore is made up of three islands: North Core Banks, South Core Banks, and Shackleford Banks. Portsmouth Island is at the northernmost point of the seashore, on North Shore Banks. This abandoned village has been preserved. Dating from the 1700s, this was once the largest community on the Outer Banks. South Core Banks is famous for its Cape Lookout Lighthouse, which overlooks the dreaded Frying Pan Shoals. The lightkeeper's quarters are currently being used by the park service as a residence for a volunteer ranger. At the most southern point, you will find Shackleford Island, the wildest of the three. Huge sand dunes meet maritime forest here. No matter which section you choose to visit, you will be enjoying one of the few uninhabited, wild beach areas left in the United States, accessible only by boat. Take your time to explore the islands, enjoying the slow pace of island time.

**TRIP HIGHLIGHTS:** Wilderness beach camping, miles and miles of beach to yourself, heaven.

**TRIP RATING:** Intermediate to advanced.

**TRIP DURATION:** Two to three hours; 7 miles.

**NAVIGATION AIDS:** USGS Map NC0313, Cape Lookout, 1:24,000.

**TIDAL INFORMATION:** There will be strong tidal influence from the inlet. Make sure you have a tide table and time your trip with the tidal movement.

Westmouth
Bay

Browns Island

Eastmouth Bay

Harkers Island

Harkers Island Road

Shell
Point

P
launch
site

Back Sound

0          1
mile

Bald
Hill
Bay

Cedar
Hammock

Morgan
Island

Lighthouse Channel

Johnsons
Bay

Cape Lookout National Seashore

Shackleford Banks

Great Marsh
Island

## CAPE LOOKOUT
◆
*National Seashore*

**CAUTIONS:** There is boat traffic in the area, so be cautious. Stay away from the inlet. There are strong currents and shoals that could be dangerous.

**TRIP PLANNING:** There are no facilities on this island. Bring everything you will need.

**LAUNCH SITE:** From Beaufort, take U.S. 70 north 10 miles to SR–1332 (Harker's Island Road). Turn right at the large National Seashore sign and continue 8.7 miles to the headquarters building and boat launch. There are several private operators who can ferry you and your kayak across. If you have a four-wheel-drive vehicle, you can have it transported too, which can help you access some of the more out-of-the-way sections of the seashore.

## DIRECTIONS:

*START:* From the launch site paddle directly south across **Back Sound.**

*MILE 1.0:* You will come to a small island. Pass to the right of this and continue south toward Shackleford Banks.

**MILE 2.5:** Pass to the left of **Cedar Hammock** and turn slightly southwest.

**MILE 3.5:** When you arrive at **Shackleford Banks,** pull your kayak up on the beach and take the time for some beachcombing or pull out a book and just lay back. When you are ready to return, retrace your route to the launch site at **Shell Point.**

## Where to Eat & Where to Stay

**RESTAURANTS** *Captain's Choice Restaurant* (252-728-7122) and *Island Restaurant* (252-728-2247) are both located on Harkers Island, a couple of miles from the launch site. **LODGING** *Beaufort Inn* (252-728-2600 or 800-726-0321) is located on Ann Street in Beaufort. *Inlet Inn* (800-554-5466) is on Front at Queen Street on the waterfront in Beaufort. **CAMPING** *Cedar Creek Campground and Marina* (252-225-9571) is located in Sealevel, which is north of Beaufort on U.S. 70. *Coastal River Campground* (252-728-5155) is just a few miles east of Beaufort on U.S. 70 in Otway.

# Blackbeard

Blackbeard is known as North Carolina's pirate, although he was not a native. He came from England and began his career as an honest seaman. His original name was Edward Drummond; once he became a pirate, he was known as Edward Teach. But to most, he will always be known as Blackbeard. His ship, *Queen Anne's Revenge,* sported forty cannon on her decks.

It was wise for a pirate to become know as fearsome, since a bad reputation helped in his line of work. Blackbeard was very good at emphasizing his evil side. He was a big man with a busy, black beard, which gave him his name. He would plait his beard into braids and, just before battle, he would light slow-burning fuses and tuck them under his hat to give a more frightful appearance. In his belt were pistols, daggers, and a cutlass. On his chest he wore a bandolier (chest harness) that held six pistols, all of which were primed and ready for firing. It's not surprising that Blackbeard was the most feared pirate on the seas.

# Bogue Banks

# Route 31:

━━ ━━ ━━ ━━ ━━ ━━ ━━ ━━ ━━ ━━ ➤

## Hammocks Beach State Park

**H**ammocks Beach has to be one of the most beautiful beaches in the area and one of the most popular spots for sea kayakers on the North Carolina Coast. This island, like many, can only be reached by boat. You can take the 2.5-mile-long ferry ride in either direction. You can camp by the shore, usually with no neighbors. Plan on camping on Bear Island, where you can camp directly on the beach.

**TRIP HIGHLIGHTS:** Camping on the beach; no cars; almost like having an island to yourself.

**TRIP RATING:** Beginner.

**TRIP DURATION:** Three to four hours; 6 miles.

**NAVIGATION AIDS:** USGS Map NC0350, Hubert, 1:24,000.

**TIDAL INFORMATION:** The tide will fluctuate up to 3 feet during the day. Check the tide table to make sure you are aware of the changing tides. Bogue Inlet can create a current when the tide is changing that can make paddling difficult if you are trying to travel against it. Plan your trip carefully.

**CAUTIONS:** Boat traffic from the Intracoastal Waterway can be hazardous.

**TRIP PLANNING:** Bring all the supplies you will need, including shade. As always, bring plenty of water and food.

**LAUNCH SITE:** From Swansboro, take NC–24 west for 2 miles until you reach SR–1511, otherwise known as Hammocks Beach Road. Turn left and drive 2.1 miles to the park entrance. The ramp is next to the parking lot.

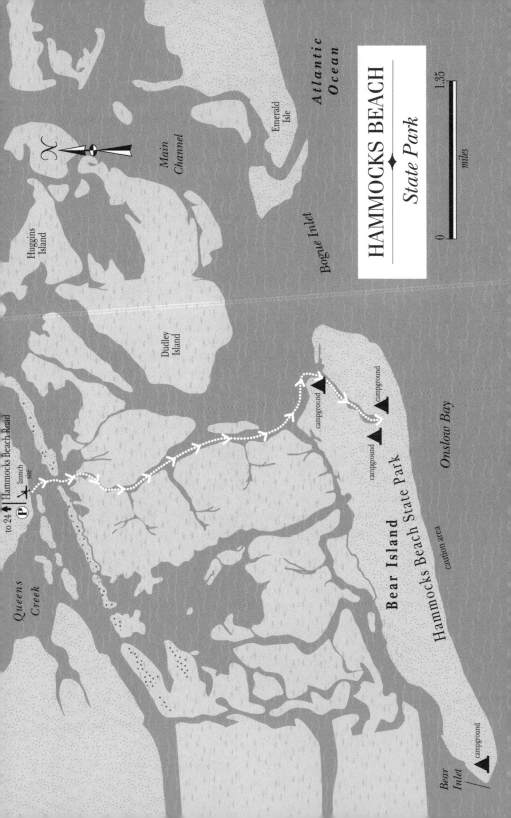

HAMMOCKS BEACH
_State Park_

0 _____ 1.35
_miles_

Atlantic Ocean

Emerald Isle

Bogue Inlet

Main Channel

Huggins Island

Dudley Island

Queens Creek

to 24 ← Hammocks Beach Road
Ⓟ  launch site

Bear Island

Hammocks Beach State Park

campground

campground

campground

campground

campground

Onslow Bay

caution area

Bear Inlet

***START:*** From the launch site, follow the marked kayak/canoe trail south.

***MILE 0.25:*** Paddle through the channel after crossing the **Intracoastal Waterway.**

***MILE 0.5:*** As you paddle the creek, keep an eye out for the numerous species of fish and shellfish that live here: crab, shrimp, flounder, sea trout, and bluefish. Many types of shorebirds feed here along the marsh's edge.

***MILE 1.0:*** The creek begins to widen here due to its close proximity to **Bogue Inlet.** You will see shallow sand bars in this area.

***MILE 2.0:*** The creek on your right, **Trout Channel,** got its name from the gray and speckled trout that can be caught here. This is the channel that leads to the Bear Island ferry dock.

***MILE 2.3:*** Turn right (southwest) into the small channel that leads to the beach. On your left is the northeast point of **Bear Island.** The maritime forest in this area is shrinking due to the migrating sand dunes and effects of Bogue Inlet. This channel was the site of the inlet in 1949. The marsh between the channel and the inlet has formed since then.

***MILE 3.0:*** Reach the end of the channel and land on Bear Island. Once you reach the beach there are fourteen family campsites and three group campsites. The campsites are spread along the beach just behind the primary dune line. They are all first-come, first-served. You will need to get a permit from the headquarters before you visit the island. There is a bathhouse and restroom a half mile from the ferry dock. I recommend that if you are staying the night, you set up camp and then explore this beach. You will find miles and miles of beautiful, deserted beach, filled with nothing but shells and solitude. When you are ready to return, follow the markers to retrace your route back to the launch site.

# Down East

Down East is the local name for the area that stretches from the North River, east of Beaufort, to Cedar Island. The land is filled with beautiful marshes, canals, and many undisturbed places. The local people used to make their living exclusively from the water, in some way or another. In a way they still do, because many of them work in the tourism industry, which caters to folks who come to enjoy the water.

## Where to Eat & Where to Stay

**RESTAURANTS** *Capt. Charlie's* (910–326–4303), located in Swansboro on Front Street, serves great seafood. *Yana's Ye Olde Drugstore Restaurant* (910–326–5510), also on Front Street in Swansboro, is the place to go for breakfast, lunch, or a milk shake. **LODGING** *Parkerton Inn* (800–393–9909) is located just north of the intersection of NC–58 and NC–24. **CAMPING** Camping at *Hammocks Beach State Park* (910–326–4881) is by permit only (secure a permit at the park office before departing for Bear Island). Camping is allowed only in designated sites.

*Hammocks Beach State Park*

# Route 32:

▬ ▬ ▬ ▬ ▬ ▬ ▬ ▬ ▬ ▬ ▬ ▬ ▬ ▬ ➤

## Masonboro Island

**M**asonboro Island is one of the components of the North Carolina National Estuarine Research Reserve System in North Carolina. The NCNERRS encourages researchers from universities and government laboratories to use the sites for their studies in an effort to learn more about estuaries.

This pristine island is sandwiched between two highly developed beaches: Wrightsville Beach to the north and Carolina Beach to the south. Luckily, it is cut off from these areas by Masonboro Inlet to the north and Carolina Beach Inlet to the south, limiting access to the island. Masonboro Island can be reached by boat only, and no vehicles are allowed on the island. There are no concessions at all; bring everything you will need.

**TRIP HIGHLIGHTS:** Almost 9 miles of undisturbed, white sand beachfront; very few people; salt marsh and mudflats provide a great habitat for wildlife.

**TRIP RATING:** Beginner.

**TRIP DURATION:** Two to three hours; 6 miles.

**NAVIGATION AIDS:** USGS Map 0833, Wrightsville Beach, 1:24,000.

**TIDAL INFORMATION:** Some tidal influence. Try to time your visit at high tide. Much of the island is mud flats, which may make paddling more difficult in low water.

**CAUTIONS:** No facilities of any kind. Pack carefully to make sure you have enough supplies.

**TRIP PLANNING:** Although you can plan your trip to circle the

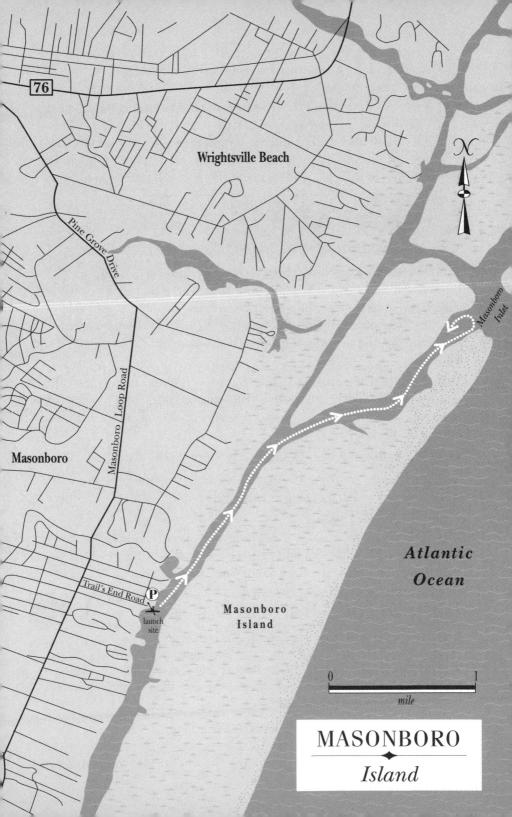

**76**

**Wrightsville Beach**

*Pine Grove Drive*

*Masonboro Loop Road*

**Masonboro**

Trail's End Road

**P**

launch
site

**Masonboro
Island**

*Masonboro Inlet*

*Atlantic
Ocean*

0              1

*mile*

# MASONBORO

◆

*Island*

entire island, this is a long trip of 18 miles and involves ocean paddling for half the trip. I recommend paddling just on the sound side and walking across to the beach.

**LAUNCH SITE:** From the intersection of U.S. 76 and NC–132 east of Wilmington, drive east on U.S. 76 0.2 mile to Pine Grove Drive. Turn right and drive 2 miles to a right turn onto Masonboro Loop Road. Continue 1.8 miles to a left turn onto Trail's End Road. Go 0.5 mile to the end of the road, where you will see the boat ramp.

**DIRECTIONS:**

**START:** From the launch site, turn right and paddle across the **Intracoastal Waterway** to **Masonboro Island.** The island is an "overwash" island: It regularly gets washed over from heavy seas and sound-side flooding. The profile is low and duneless; more than three-quarters of the island is mudflat and salt marsh. Turn left to paddle north along the shoreline.

**MILE 1.0:** The extensive marsh area here is very important to the fishing industry. The marsh grass, constantly fluctuating tides, and warm shallow waters are very important in supporting and providing refuge for much marine wildlife.

**MILE 1.5:** Follow the island's shore as it bends northeast.

**MILE 2.0:** There are some shrub thickets directly behind the dune line. Work your way north, keeping as close as possible to the shore without grounding on the flats.

**MILE 3.0:** When you reach the northernmost point of Masonboro Island, take time to get out and explore the beach. When ready to return, retrace your route back to the launch site.

## Where to Eat & Where to Stay

**RESTAURANTS** *King Neptune* (910–256–2525) on Lumina Avenue in Wrightsville Beach serves great seafood. *Manhattan Bagel* (910–256–1222) on Wrightsville Avenue in Wrightsville Beach sells bagels with all the fixings. **LODGING** *Summer Sands Motel* (910–256–4175 or 800–336–4849) is located on Lumina Avenue in Wrightsville Beach. **CAMPING** *Carolina Beach State Park* (910–458–8206), on Dow Road 1 mile north of Carolina Beach, is just minutes from Masonboro Inlet and Cape Fear River.

# Sneads Ferry

When I graduated from high school, a group of us decided to have a grand adventure in Cape Hatteras National Seashore, so we rented a house in Buxton. We wanted to pick up some fireworks at South of the Border, which is a roadside attraction on I–95 just across the border in South Carolina. Being the experienced world travelers that we were, we looked at the map and decided that we could drive down I–95 from Washington, D.C., to South of the Border, then cut over and take a ferry at Sneads Ferry, North Carolina. Sneads Ferry is a small town just off U.S. 17, north of Wilmington. This would get us up to the ferry at Cedar Island, which would take us to Ocracoke, where we would take another ferry to Hatteras and to our rental house. We drove to Sneads Ferry and spent an hour looking for the ferry. We decided to ask for directions from a man sitting in a chair outside a gas station (he had been watching us drive around and around). He just looked at us with a very patient look and said, "There ain't no ferry in Sneads Ferry. Why don't you just drive over the bridge?" Well, needless to say, we felt humbled after that, and learned to read a map better.

# Route 33:

## *Fort Fisher*

**L**ive oaks with limbs seared by the salty wind and spray, the ocean visible in the background—this is Fort Fisher. Located on the southern tip of Pleasure Island near Wilmington, 5 miles south of Carolina Beach, Fort Fisher tapers to a point, with the Atlantic Ocean on the east and Cape Fear River on the west. You'll find miles of white sand beach, salt marsh, tidal creeks, the North Carolina Aquarium, and of course, the fort.

**TRIP HIGHLIGHTS:** Salt marsh, tidal creeks, and mudflats teeming with wading birds and other wildlife; 3 miles of beach.

**TRIP RATING:** Beginner.

**TRIP DURATION:** 2 hours to all day; 2 miles.

**NAVIGATION AIDS:** USGS Maps NC0102, Carolina Beach, and NC0833, Wrightsville Beach, 1:24,000.

**TIDAL INFORMATION:** The tides will fluctuate up to 4 feet depending on the time of day. Make sure you have a tide chart and plan your trip accordingly.

**CAUTIONS:** This route is located in the Cape Fear River. Keep an eye out for boat traffic.

**TRIP PLANNING:** Make this trip only during a falling tide, which is the only time the "Rocks" are passable.

**LAUNCH SITE:** From Kure Beach, follow U.S. 421 southwest for 4 miles until it ends at the ferry dock, where you will find the public boat launch.

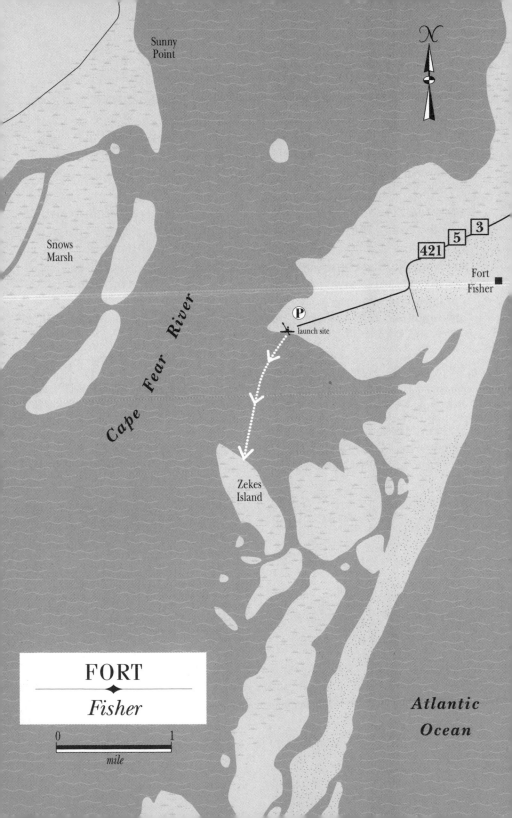

Sunny
Point

Snows
Marsh

*Cape Fear River*

421 5 3

Fort
Fisher

P
launch site

Zekes
Island

**FORT**
*Fisher*

0                    1

*mile*

*Atlantic
Ocean*

N

**START:** From the launch site head south across the Cape Fear River to a breakwater known as **"the Rocks."** It was built to prevent shoaling in the river. Inside the rocks is a bay of water called "the Basin." Follow the breakwater until you reach a small, sandy spit that has some small shrubs growing on it.

**MILE 1.0:** **Zeke's Island** is a 1,165-acre preserve that is part of the North Carolina National Estuarine Research Preserve. Covered by tidal flats, shallow waters, and barrier spit, this preserve is an important habitat for the loggerhead sea turtle and many shorebirds. Being secluded has helped the bird population thrive. Many species breed here, including the brown pelican, which can be found in very large numbers. After you have explored Zeke's Island by foot, return to your kayak and head back out to the Rocks and back to the launch site.

## Where to Eat & Where to Stay

**RESTAURANTS** *Big Daddy's Seafood Restaurant* (910–458–8622) on K Avenue in Kure Beach is a Kure Beach tradition for seafood "Calabash style." **LODGING** *Seven Seas Inn* (910–458–8122) is on Ft. Fisher Boulevard in Kure Beach. **CAMPING** *Carolina Beach State Park* (910–458–8206), on Dow Road 1 mile north of Carolina Beach, is just minutes from Masonboro Inlet and Cape Fear River.

# Route 34:

━ ━ ━ ━ ━ ━ ━ ━ ━ ━ ━ ━ ━ ━ ➤

## Bald Head Island

**B**arely 2 miles off the southeastern tip of North Carolina lies a semitropical island. Covered by dunes and beach, maritime forest, and vast salt marshes, this secluded island is a paddler's paradise. There is no bridge to the island, so you won't see any cars, but you will see golf carts. You can paddle across or take the passenger ferry from Southport.

Development of the island initially created much controversy, but the existing resort has become self-sustaining, with the island's mix of forests and marsh the focal point. Although Bald Head Island is known as a private resort, anyone can visit and rent a cottage, room, or villa.

The 14 miles of pristine beach attract visitors of another kind, the sea turtles that nest here. Bald Head Island is the principal loggerhead sea turtle rookery. The nesting season runs June through August, with the hatchlings emerging approximately sixty days from nesting. Also located on Bald Head is the Bald Head Island State Natural Area. The park encompasses more than 10,000 acres and is managed by the North Carolina Division of Parks and Recreation.

**TRIP HIGHLIGHTS:** Gorgeous beaches, no cars, very low-impact housing.

**TRIP RATING:** Intermediate if you take the ferry, advanced if you paddle from Southport.

**TRIP DURATION:** Four to six hours; 7.5 miles.

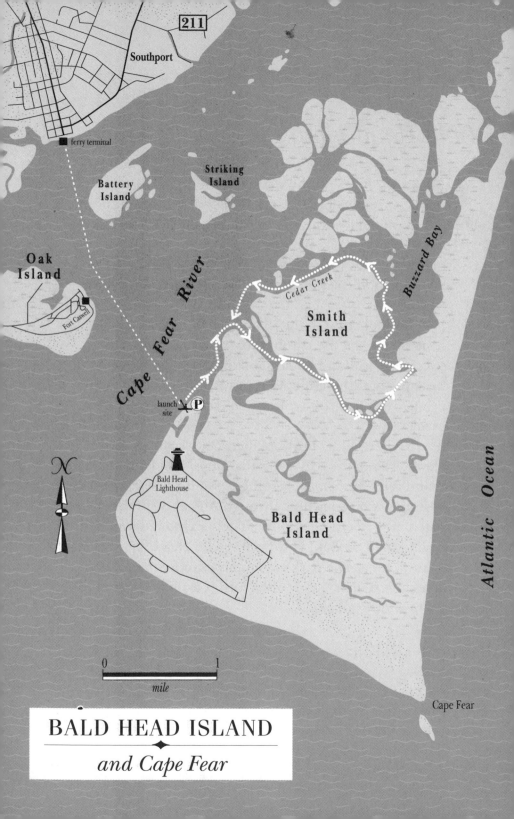

Southport

211

ferry terminal

Battery
Island

Striking
Island

Oak
Island

Fort Caswell

Cape Fear River

Cedar Creek

Smith
Island

Buzzard Bay

launch
site

P

Bald Head
Lighthouse

Bald Head
Island

N

Atlantic Ocean

0 _____ 1
*mile*

Cape Fear

# BALD HEAD ISLAND
## *and Cape Fear*

**NAVIGATION AIDS:** USGS Maps NC0385, Kure Beach, and NC0099, Cape Fear, 1:24,000.

**TIDAL INFORMATION:** Cape Fear has a strong tidal influence. Pick up a tide table before you leave Southport.

**CAUTIONS:** Cape Fear Inlet is a huge inlet, appropriately named. It is famous for its currents and shoals. Even though it is only 3 miles from Southport to Bald Head, I recommend taking the ferry.

**TRIP PLANNING:** Take the ferry from Indigo Plantation instead of paddling to Bald Head Island. It's only $14 and well worth the money in safety and time.

**LAUNCH SITE:** From Route 211 South (Howe Street) in Southport, turn right onto West Ninth Street. Follow this road 1.7 miles to Indigo Plantation Drive, which dead-ends at the ferry terminal. After a twenty-minute ferry ride you will land at the town marina, where you can put in.

# DIRECTIONS:

**START:** From the launch site, turn right and head north. This will take you away from the Cape Fear Inlet and into the more protected marsh area called Smith Island, which is actually a group of smaller islands.

**MILE 0.5:** On your right will be a channel. Keep paddling past this until you reach the next one.

**MILE 1.0:** You will see the second channel on your right. Turn here and follow it as it winds through the marsh.

**MILE 1.5:** When you come to the fork in the creek, keep to your left and continue paddling down the channel (east).

**MILE 2.5:** Stay to the left as the channel curves to your left here.

**MILE 3.25:** Enter **Buzzard Bay,** keep to your left, and follow the shoreline as it winds north.

**MILE 4.0:** Keep to your left and follow the shore as it winds west.

**MILE 4.5:** Turn left into **Cedar Creek** and paddle southwest along the shoreline.

**MILE 5.5:** Turn left at Cape Fear River and paddle 2 miles back to the launch site, which will be on your left.

## *Where to Eat & Where to Stay*

For information on Bald Head Island restaurants and accommodations contact the Bald Head Island Club at (800) 432–RENT. See Route 35, Oak Island, for restaurants, lodging, and camping in the Southport area.

*Bald Head Island*

# Route 35:

━ ━━ ━━ ━━ ━━ ━━ ━━ ━━ ━━ ━━ ━━ ━▶

## Oak Island

**O**ak Island's 13-mile beachfront incorporates the communities of Caswell Beach, Yaupon Beach, and Long Beach. Fort Caswell lies on the most northern section of the island. This earthworks fort was constructed in 1826 to guard the entrance to the Cape Fear River. It was captured by Confederates in 1861, and was used again during the Spanish-American War and both world wars. It currently overlooks the Cape Fear River's more sedate boat traffic.

**TRIP HIGHLIGHTS:**  The Oak Island Lighthouse, Fort Caswell, and the sound-side marshes.

**TRIP RATING:**  Beginner.

**TRIP DURATION:**  Three to four hours; 3 miles.

**NAVIGATION AIDS:**  USGS Map NC0704, Southport, 1:24,000.

**TIDAL INFORMATION:**  The tidal fluctuation will be from 3 to 4 feet, depending on the wind. Make sure you have a tide chart and plan your trip accordingly.

**CAUTIONS:**  Stay south of the Cape Fear River. Strong tidal influence and ship traffic can be dangerous.

**TRIP PLANNING:**  This is an open area, so keep an eye out for boat traffic. The Cape Fear Inlet can be hazardous depending on the weather. Make sure you know the weather and tides and plan your trip carefully.

**LAUNCH SITE:**  Cross the Intracoastal Waterway on NC–133 and turn left onto Caswell Road. Follow the road past the Oak Island Lighthouse. There is a public boat ramp off to the left with a small parking area.

# DIRECTIONS:

**START:** From the launch site, follow the narrow channel for 0.5 mile until it intersects with the **Cape Fear River.**

**MILE 0.5:** Turn right and follow the shore until you reach **Fort Caswell.**

**MILE 1.5:** On your right is a small cove, which is great for bird-watching and viewing Fort Caswell. Once you have explored as long as you wish, head back to your left for 1 mile.

**MILE 2.5:** Turn left into the channel and return to the launch site.

## Where to Eat & Where to Stay

**RESTAURANTS** If you're tired of seafood, try *Thai Peppers* (910–457–0095) on East Moore Street in Southport. **LODGING** *Sea Captain Motor Lodge* (910–457–5263) is on West West Street in Southport. **CAMPING** *Long Beach Family Campground* (910–278–5737), on East Oak Island Drive in Long Beach, is just minutes from Oak Island.

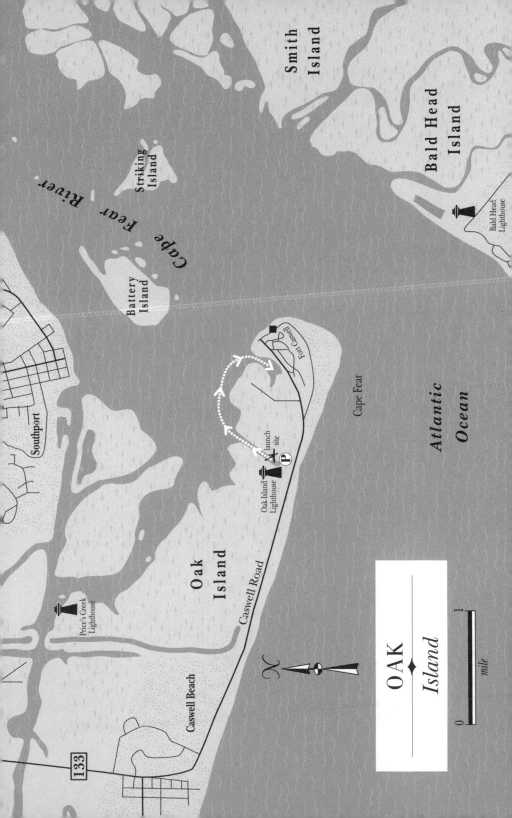

# Appendix A

## Paddlesports Rentals, Tours, Sales, and Instruction

*Note:* Codes follow each establishment to indicate some of the services provided: paddlesport rentals ( R ), tours ( T ), sales ( S ), and instruction ( I ).

### Northern Outer Banks

**Kitty Hawk Kayaks,** P.O. Box 939, Nags Head, NC 27959; (252) 261–0145 (R, T, S, I)

**Kitty Hawk Sports,** P.O. Box 939, Nags Head, NC 27959; (252) 441–6800 or (800) 948–0759; info@khsports.com, www.khsports.com (R, T, S, I)

**Ocracoke Adventures,** Silver Lake Road, Ocracoke, NC 27960; (252) 928–7873 (R, T, I)

**Wilderness Canoeing,** P.O. Box 789, Manteo, NC 27954; (252) 473–1960 (T)

### Southern Outer Banks

**AB Kayaks,** 328 Front Street, Beaufort, NC 28516; (252) 728–6330 or (252) 877–KAYAKNC; www.ABKayaks.com; (R, T, I)

**Island Rigs,** Mile Marker 12.5, NC–58, 1980 Salterpath Road, Indian Beach, NC 28512; (252) 247–7787; (R, T, S, I)

**Pro Canoe and Kayak,** 435 Eastwood Road, Wilmington, NC 28403; (910) 256–1258; also located in Raleigh and Greensboro; (R, T, S, I)

# Appendix B

## National and State Parks, Refuges, Museums, and Reserves

*Note:* Mailing addresses, rather than physical addresses, are given. Please call for information and directions.

**Alligator River National Wildlife Refuge,** P.O. Box 1969, Manteo, NC 27954; (252) 473–1131

**Bald Head Island State Natural Area,** Coastal Reserve Coordinator, 7205 Wrightsville Avenue, Wilmington, NC 28403; (910) 256–3721

**Cape Hatteras National Seashore,** Route 1, Box 675, Manteo, NC 27954; (252) 473–2111

**Cape Lookout National Seashore,** 131 Charles Street, Harkers Island, NC 28531; (910) 728–2250

**Carolina Beach State Park,** P.O. Box 475, Carolina Beach, NC 28428; (910) 458–8206

**Cedar Island National Wildlife Refuge,** Cedar Island, NC 28520; (910) 225–2511

**Coastal Reserve Coordinator,** North Carolina National Estuarine Research Reserve, 7205 Wrightsville Avenue, Wilmington, NC 28403; (910) 256–3721

**Currituck Beach Lighthouse and Lightkeeper's Quarters,** Outer Banks Conservationists, Inc., P.O. Box 361, Corolla, NC 27927; (252) 453–4939

**Currituck National Wildlife Refuge,** P.O. Box 39, Knotts Island, NC 27950; (252) 429–3100

**Division of Coastal Management,** North Carolina Department of Natural Resources and Community Development, P.O. Box 27687, Raleigh, NC 27687; (919) 733–2293

**Elizabeth II State Historic Site,** P.O. Box 155, Manteo, NC 27954; (252) 473–1144

**Fort Fisher State Historic Area,** P.O. Box 68, Kure Beach, NC 28449; (910) 458–5538

**Fort Macon State Park,** P.O. Box 127, Atlantic Beach, NC 28512; (910) 726–3775

**Fort Raleigh National Historic Site,** Route 1, Box 675, Manteo, NC 27954; (252) 473–2111

**Hammocks Beach State Park,** Route 2, Box 295, Swansboro, NC 28584; (910) 326–4881

**Jockey's Ridge State Park,** P.O. Box 27959, Nags Head, NC 27959; (252) 441–7132

**Lake Mattamuskeet National Wildlife Refuge,** Route 1, Box N-2, Swan Quarter, NC 27885; (252) 926–4021

**Nags Head Woods Preserve,** 701 West Ocean Acres Drive, Kill Devil Hills, NC 27948; (252) 441–2525

**North Carolina Aquarium:**

Fort Fisher, P.O. Box 130, Kure Beach, NC 28449; (910) 459–8257

Pine Knoll Shores, P.O. Box 580, Atlantic Beach, NC 28512; (910) 247–4003

Roanoke Island, P.O. Box 967, Manteo, NC 27954; (252) 473–3493

**Pea Island National Wildlife Refuge,** P.O. Box 150, Rodanthe, NC 27968; (252) 987–2394

**Theodore Roosevelt State Natural Area,** P.O. Box 127, Atlantic Beach, NC 28512; (910) 726–3775

**Wright Brothers National Memorial,** Route 1, Box 675, Manteo, NC 27954; (252) 473–2111

# Appendix C

## Local Events

**Bogue Sound Kayak Festival,** Indian Beach, early August. Kayak race, demos, clinics. (252) 247–7787.

**OBX Oceanfest,** Nags Head, last weekend in August. Surf kayak competition, Hawaiian outrigger race, kayak and surf ski race, demos, clinics. (252) 441–2756.

# Appendix D

## Paddling Clubs

**Carolina Canoe Club,** P.O. Box 12932, Raleigh, NC 27605

**Outer Banks Paddlers,** 1004 West Kitty Hawk Road, Kitty Hawk, NC 27949

# Appendix E

## Recommended Reading

Angier, Bradford. *Field Guide to Edible Wild Plants.* Harrisburg, PA: Stackpole Books, 1974.

Corsa, E.M., and Linda Lauby. *Insiders' Guide to North Carolina's Outer Banks.* Helena, MT: Falcon Publishing, Inc., 2000.

Eastman, John. *The Book of Swamp and Bog.* Mechanicsburg, PA: Stackpole Books, 1995.

Goldstein, Robert J. *Coastal Fishing in the Carolinas.* Winston-Salem, NC: John F. Blair, Publisher, 2000.

Kopper, Philip. *The Wild Edge.* New York: Quandrangle/The New York Times Book Co., Inc., 1979.

Kraus, E. Jean Wilson. *A Guide to Ocean Dune Plants Common to North Carolina.* Chapel Hill: The University of North Carolina Press, 1988.

Meyer, Peter. *Nature Guide to the Carolina Coast.* Wilmington, NC: Avian-Cetacean Press, 1998.

Morris, Glen. *North Carolina Beaches.* Chapel Hill: The University of North Carolina Press, 1993.

Pilkey, Orrin H., Jr., William J. Neal, & Orrin H. Pilkey Sr. *From Currituck to Calabash.* Research Triangle Park, NC: The North Carolina Science and Technology Research Center, 1982.

Petry, Loren C. and Marcia G. Norman. *A Beachcomber's Botany.* Chatham, MA: The Chatham Conservation Foundation, Inc., 1992.

Sylvestre, Jean-Pierre. *Dolphins & Porpoises.* New York: Sterling Publishing, Co., Inc., 1993.

Tate, Ruth S. *Bring Me Duck.* Nags Head, NC: Nags Head Art, 1986.

Stick, David. *The Outer Banks of North Carolina.* Chapel Hill: The University of North Carolina Press, 1990.

Tiner, Ralph W. *Field Guide to Coastal Wetland Plants of the Southeastern United States.* Amherst, MA: The University of Massachusetts Press, 1993.

# About the Author

Pamela Malec has been kayaking for twenty-five years. She is actively involved in all types of paddling, including sea kayaking, canoeing, surf ski, outrigger, wild water, whitewater, and surf kayaking. She has been teaching sea kayaking and surf kayaking on the Outer Banks since 1983. Considered one of the leading authorities nationally on surf kayaking, she recently wrote the curriculum for the ACA's Surf Kayaking Instruction Course. Pam is a current board member of the American Canoe Association National Board of Directors and is a member of the Safety, Education and Instruction Council. Cochairman of the National Surf Kayaking Committee, she travels around the country competing and helping to promote the various paddlesports competitions.

Pam started working as the Kayak Program Director for Kitty Hawk Sports, located in Nags Head, North Carolina, five years ago. She is currently the General Manager for Kitty Hawk Watersports, a division of Kitty Hawk Sports.

Pam has traveled to California, Florida, Mexico, Central America, and the Caribbean, paddling, researching, and leading trips. She has written articles on paddling the Outer Banks for local travel guides and other publications. She is in tune with the simple pleasure of paddling and loves to share her knowledge and passion for the sport.

## Experience the exhilaration of kayaking the North Carolina coast

"Very comprehensive and fun to read . . . a good guidebook that is so descriptive, so evocative, and so complete that you'll have trouble putting it down to actually go take a trip!"

—Joe Miller, Outdoor Columnist, The RALEIGH NEWS & OBSERVER

GUIDE TO SEA KAYAKING NORTH CAROLINA lets kayakers of all skill levels explore 35 trips in some of the most spectacular and wildlife-rich marine habitats on the planet.

Designed for beginner, intermediate, and advanced kayakers, this guide gives mile-by-mile descriptions of the routes, including prominent landmarks and interesting sights along the way. Detailed maps and overviews of North Carolina's weather, tide, and current patterns complete this first major treatment of paddling this spectacular coastline.

### Complete trip planning information:

✔ skill levels for each route
✔ detailed maps
✔ launching and landing sites
✔ sidetrip options
✔ navigational aids
✔ wildlife and local lore
✔ camping, lodging, and restaurants

**Discover day trips and tours to**
Roanoke Island ▪ Ocracoke ▪ Alligator River National Wildlife Refuge ▪ Cape Hatteras National Seashore ▪ Bald Head Island

This book is a must for anyone paddling the North Carolina coast, whether exploring quiet, bird-filled estuaries and protected bays or navigating around the Outer Banks.

The Globe Pequot Press

Guilford, CT 06437
www.globe-pequot.com